Contents

Section Two: Strategies and Support for Undergraduate and Postgraduate Teaching and Learning

Notes on Contributors

Maxine Alterio, John Waddick and **Pamela Wood** are at the Otago Polytechnic, Dunedin, New Zealand. Maxine is Staff Development Coordinator, interested in reflective mechanisms to enhance professional practice. Pamela is Assistant to Director (Research) and Staff Development Coordinator. John is an educational technologist interested in using multimedia for learning purposes.

Jan Bamforth is at the Business School, University of North London.

Clare Brindley is Course Leader of two undergraduate programmes at Crewe and Alsager Faculty of Manchester Metropolitan University. She lectures in the area of marketing strategy and her current research interests involve leisure marketing and teaching and learning strategies in higher education.

Sally Brown is based in the Educational Development Service at the University of Northumbria at Newcastle. She is Chair of the SEDA publications committee and runs staff development workshops in the UK and overseas. She has written extensively on educational development and teaching issues, including *Assessing Learners in Higher Education* and *Research, Teaching and Learning in Higher Education*.

Peter Cuthbert is Course Leader of the BA (Hons) Business Administration at Crewe and Alsager Faculty of Manchester Metropolitan University. He lectures at the university in the areas of quantitative techniques, data processing and research methods. His current research interest is in student approaches to study and academic success. Peter is Convenor of the Association of Business Schools' Undergraduate Course Leaders' Network.

Steve Fallows is Reader in Education Development and Research Supervisors Coordinator at the Centre for Educational Development, University of Luton. He is co-editing a book on modularization and semesterization, due to be published by Kogan Page.

John Goodfellow is at the Business School, University of North London.

Michael Gregory is Dean of Business and Management and Director of Suffolk Management Development Centre at Suffolk College – an associate college of the University of East Anglia.

Keith Guest is Head of the Study Skills team in the Educational Services Unit at the University of Luton.

Liz McDowell is Senior Lecturer in Educational Development at the University of Northumbria, Newcastle. She has directed a number of research and evaluation projects with particular emphasis on student experiences and perspectives.

Deanna C Martin is International Director of Supplemental Instruction and Director of the Center for Academic Development at the University of Missouri, Kansas City. **F Kim Wilcox**, also at the University of Missouri, is Director of Training for Supplemental Instruction.

Erica Morris was Assistant Enterprise Officer within the School of Biological Sciences, University of Sussex, from 1993–95. She is particularly interested in computer-based learning and interface design. She has recently moved to the Institute of Education Technology at the Open University. At the time their work was undertaken, both Erica and Mike Tribe were funded by the Enterprise Development Fund and the Teaching and Learning Development Fund.

Lyn Oates is Learning and Teaching Support Manager at the Cheltenham and Gloucester College of Higher Education.

Vivienne Rivis is Assistant Director, Quality Enhancement and Quality Assurance at the Higher Education Quality Council with responsibility for work on student guidance and support.

Robert Simpson is a Senior Lecturer at the University of East London, where he works in the Learning Development Unit, which has responsibility for promoting learning development entitlement across the university. Previously he has worked abroad and in secondary education and adult further and higher education.

Ian Solomonides and **Malcolm Swannell** are in the Department of Mechanical Engineering at Nottingham Trent University. Ian, a Primary Art and Design graduate, has worked for the department since 1992, when he was initially employed to develop student study skills. He is now Lecturer and First Year Tutor, responsible for the induction and ongoing support of all new entrants. Malcolm graduated in 1972 from the Mechanical Engineering Department, in which he is now Senior Lecturer and Final Year Tutor. His research interests include Engineering Education and Biomechanical Engineering. Ian and Malcolm have been instrumental in the change in teaching practice now evident within the department.

Nick Sutcliffe is a researcher and part-time lecturer in the School of Human and Health Sciences at the University of Huddersfield. His research interests include student learning and assessment in higher professional education.

Dr Mike Tribe is Senior Lecturer in the School of Biological Sciences and Science Liaison Director for the University of Sussex. He has been involved with several undergraduate teaching and learning projects since 1970 and has run several workshops in developing countries as well as advising on many aspects of biological education in the UK and Europe. At the time their work was undertaken, both Mike and Erica Morris were funded by the Enterprise Development Fund and the Teaching and Learning Development Fund.

Les Watson is Dean of Information Services, Faculty of Information Services, at the Cheltenham and Gloucester College of Higher Education.

Tony Wailey is APEL and Mature Student Advisor at the Centre for Access, Advice and Continuing Education at the University of East London. Previously he has worked in guidance centres and adult further and higher education. He has published in many fields, particularly in relation to the demands and concerns of adult learners.

Annette Wilson and **Steve Wilson** are at the University of Portsmouth. Annette is Principal Lecturer in software engineering and is Director of the computer studies degree scheme, which has over 500 students. Steve is Senior Lecturer in computer hardware and Senior Admissions Tutor and Degree Stream Manager recruiting about 400 new students each year.

Gina Wisker is Adviser for Staff Development at Anglia Polytechnic University. She is a member of the consultancy team at the Oxford Centre for Staff Development and a member of the Staff and Education Development Executive and Publications committees. She co-edits *Innovations in Education and Training International* with Chris Bell and is the author and co-author of many books, including *What's So Special About Women in Higher Education?*, *Supporting More Students* and *Assessing More Students*.

Preface

A fundamental concern within higher education today is to ensure that strategies are in place to provide systematic guidance and support for students in order to enable them to learn. With increasing numbers of students, a diverse student population coming from a wide variety of learning backgrounds and decreasing per capita funding, there are grave concerns that the student learning experience as a whole is being threatened.

This book explores a range of strategies, both institutional and individual which have been developed by academic and support staff to foster the kind of context, atmosphere, facilities and attitudes in relation to learning which support students who are learning in universities. Student services and central systems available to students under modular systems are particularly addressed here.

The contributors, many of whom participated in the Staff and Educational Development Association conference on Enabling Student Learning at Worthing in November 1994, examine in this book how best to enable all kinds of students to make the most of opportunities for learning available in higher education. The book includes references to computer-aided support systems as well as to the range of ways in which personal and peer tutoring systems can help to make the student experience rewarding and successful.

Students nowadays invest highly in their university education, both in terms of effort and of finance, often graduating with high levels of debt. In order to enable them to get the most from their experience in higher education, we need to ensure that they obtain the best possible support available. This book addresses how we can do this, within the limitations and constraints of our current working context.

Gina Wisker &
Sally Brown,
November 1995

SECTION ONE:
Systems and Structures
to Enable Student Learning

Chapter 1

Assuring the Quality of Guidance and Learner Support in Higher Education

Vivienne Rivis

INTRODUCTION

This chapter reviews recent developments in guidance and learner support in the UK higher education sector and describes an approach to quality assurance developed by the Higher Education Quality Council, based on a set of quality assurance guidelines. The chapter also considers the potential impact of guidance and learner support on the maintenance of academic standards. Some of the material in this chapter has already appeared in an article in the Employment Department's *Network News*, Edition 1, February 1995.

The HE sector in the UK has had an ambivalent attitude to guidance and learner support. On the one hand there has been a persistent view that students entering HE ought, by virtue of their academic abilities, to be able to make effective decisions about learning, to deal with academic and personal problems without recourse to specialist help and to operate more or less as autonomous learners. On the other hand, the tradition of personal tutoring established by the ancient universities and adopted subsequently by both old and new universities has implicitly acknowledged that HE students derive both academic and personal benefits from one-to-one academic guidance. Moreover, in recent years, the expansion of university counselling and careers advisory services in the old universities, and of multi-specialist student services in the new universities, has demonstrated a recognition that HE students require a range of academic, personal and practical services to enable them to derive full benefit from their programmes of learning.

CHANGE AND ITS CONSEQUENCES

Recent innovations in the organization and delivery of guidance and learner support cannot be considered without a review of the context of educational change in which they are rooted. The steady expansion of HE from the mid-1960s was brought into sudden focus by the government-engineered rapid expansion of the late 1980s and early 1990s. This coincided with the reform of the entire post-school sector, severing the link between non-university institutions and the local authorities, and with the creation of new funding mechanisms for a unitary HE sector (HEFCE, 1994). However, rapid expansion was followed by abrupt 'consolidation' with the introduction of financial penalties for over-recruitment, and incentives through the Funding Councils to encourage universities to offer economically-valued subjects such as science and engineering.

Government policy was mirrored by significant changes in patterns of entry to HE. Although the expansion of participation in HE has led to a much higher proportion of young people undertaking university-level study, the apparent expansion has been amongst 'mature' students, particularly women, reflecting the success of the Access, educational guidance and the equal opportunities movements of the 1970s and 1980s (FEU, 1994; HEFCE, 1994). Increasing numbers of students study part-time, often while working, and there has been a corresponding expansion of continuing professional development programmes.

Changes in the numbers and characteristics of HE students have been accompanied by changes in the way their education is organized and delivered. The majority of universities and increasing numbers of colleges have moved towards more flexible, credit-based programmes, often linked to modularization of the curriculum and the replacement of the three traditional terms with two or more semesters (Robertson, 1994). Students are now more likely to be viewed as autonomous learners, and academic staff are expected to pay much greater attention to the quality of their teaching and the effectiveness of their students' learning (Imeson, 1995).

Students, faced with a very wide choice of learning options at the beginning of, and sometimes throughout, their learning programmes are seeking help from both academic and administrative staff in making decisions about their individual learning pathways. There is a widespread view that the expansion of student numbers has meant that personal tutor systems have been put under enormous strain and in many institutions have in fact collapsed.

Universities and colleges have been examining other models of support for students, including group and peer tutoring, or the use of programme advisers, to compensate for the lack of one-to-one tutoring (HEQC, 1994b; Moore, 1995). The weakening of this individualized, personal link between tutor and student has other concomitants, notably a widespread view that students are adopting an increasingly consumerist attitude to their education, reflecting the influence of the market on institutions, their corporate customers, the employers, and the 'consumers' of education, the students. Students appear more likely to appeal against unsatisfactory assessments, or to complain about other issues regarding the quality of their learning experience. This increased consumerism is accompanied by changes which have rendered students, especially part-time students, the direct purchasers of their own learning services.

The increasingly difficult financial situation of many students and their families and the inability of most institutions to alleviate those difficulties has created further tensions. Retention rates are giving cause for concern in many institutions (Moore, 1995) especially where high dropout appears to be linked to financial hardship. This has been acknowledged by the funding bodies: the Chief Executive of the HEFCE has noted that students who cannot afford to study full-time often return to part-time HE where, incidentally, there are no sources of financial assistance (Davies, 1995).

One of the main criticisms of credit-based and modular programmes is their fragmentary nature – for both staff and students. Students, especially those studying part-time or off-campus at work or at home through distance learning or discontinuously, may feel themselves to be isolated and lacking in the peer group support available through the traditional three-year full-time single honours programme (Moore, 1995; HEQC, 1994b).

Equally, academic staff may regret the more limited opportunities to develop close rapport with a group of students over an extended period. Institutions have been actively addressing these issues, recognizing that expansion and diversity have created a different set of challenges about the organization of teaching and learning, and the quality of the students' experience, which are not simply related to the accommodation of greater numbers of students.

In fact, the HE sector has a strong track record in some aspects of innovative practice in guidance about learning. The Open University embedded the notion of academic counselling in its delivery structures from an early stage and went on to encourage and support the establishment of educational guidance services for adults (Butler, 1984). Other polytechnics and universities also contributed to the establishment of such services (Rivis, 1991). Professional associations emerged to service the interests of groups of specialist staff, such as the Association of Graduate Careers Advisory Services (AGCAS), the Association of Student Counsellors (ASC) and the Association of Managers of Student Services in Higher Education (AMOSSHE). However, as these groupings emerged there was a tendency for demarcations between specialists to increase (Watts, 1994) and for overall issues of guidance and learner support across the whole of an institution to be neglected.

In 1989, two bodies with an interest in both HE and educational guidance, the Council for National Academic Awards (CNAA) and the Unit for the

Development of Adult Continuing Education (UDACE) devised a project to examine the provision of guidance and counselling to the UK HE sector, with a particular emphasis on the experience of non-traditional and mature students. The project, which ran from 1990 to 1992, found that HE institutions had extensive guidance and counselling provision, involving a wide range of academic and non-academic staff, but that few institutions had integrated systems or institution-wide policies and plans for guidance (Herrington and Rivis *et al.*, 1994).

The UDACE/CNAA project was funded by the then Employment Department which, since the late 1980s, has acknowledged the critical role played by guidance in education and training. The focus of much Employment Department-funded guidance activity has emphasized the relationship between guidance and economic roles. For example, the National Institute for Careers and Educational Counselling (NICEC) undertook a study of careers education and the curriculum in HE, as part of the Employment Department's evaluation of its Enterprise in Higher Education Programme (Watts and Hawthorn, 1992). More recently, the Department has focused on the relationship between guidance in HE and the development of learning autonomy by supporting development projects in seven HE institutions, where a major focus is the construction and implementation of institution-wide strategies for guidance and learner support. Institutions have thus been provided with some forums for debate and opportunities for development, mainly by government sponsorship. The professional associations have tended to argue from their specific perspectives, whether it be student counselling or careers guidance, rather than across the field as a whole. Other research and development projects have referred to student or educational guidance, but in a relatively partial or undifferentiated way. For example, the government-sponsored Credit Accumulation and Transfer Development Project managed by the HEQC focused on information systems and education guidance in support of credit-based learning, although making broad recommendations about the organization of guidance and learner support in a diverse, expanded system (Robertson, 1994).

Until recently, therefore, despite the increased interest in and activity around guidance and learner support issues, there was no over-arching framework wherein HE institutions could locate their provision and against which they could assure themselves of the quality of their services. It was this gap that the HEQC has sought to fill.

QUALITY ASSURANCE OF GUIDANCE AND LEARNER SUPPORT

The HEQC, established by statute in 1992 but owned by the HE sector itself, is charged with 'contributing to the maintenance and improvement of quality, at all levels, in institutions of Higher Education in the United Kingdom'. Furthermore, 'HEQC seeks to promote public confidence in the standing and quality of the universities and colleges and the programmes and awards they offer, thereby protecting institutions' autonomy in setting and maintaining academic standards'.

Through its main functions of *quality assurance and quality enhancement,* HEQC acts with and on behalf of the universities and colleges. Thus HEQC carries out regular auditing of the ways institutions discharge their responsibilities for standards and quality and at the same time has undertaken a range of quality enhancement projects in collaboration with the institutions themselves. These projects complement the audit process by disseminating good practice through seminars, reports, discussion papers and guidelines. The *Guidelines on Quality Assurance* (HEQC, 1994a) offer an overall framework for quality assurance, based on previous CVCP and CNAA guidance. Forthcoming guidelines on credit rating will provide a more detailed framework for institutions working to enhance the quality of their credit-based learning programmes. Complementing both of these, and HEQC's *Notes for the Guidance of Auditors* (1995b) are the new Guidelines for *Guidance and Learner Support in Higher Education* (HEQC, l995a).

The idea is not new. Professional associations and individual institutions have in recent years published a string of codes of practice, statements of entitlement and good practice checklists. The *Charters for Higher Education* (DfE, 1993), have in turn stimulated institutions to produce their own charters and statements of entitlement to the teaching, learning and support services deemed to be part of the HE experience. Students and prospective students are now more likely to be offered an explicit statement of what they can expect in terms of teaching and learning, and the support services available in the institution of their choice.

However, only limited attention has been paid to the full range of guidance and practical services which are needed to underpin and facilitate HE learning, particularly in an increasingly flexible credit-based, modularized system. During exploratory work on credit and access, HEQC was asked to provide more specific assistance to institutions grappling with these issues.

In response, in Autumn 1993 HEQC set up a quality assurance Network for Guidance and Learner Support, drawn from 15 different institutions, mainly in the North of England. This group, whose members included staff and student representatives with a diverse range of academic and learner support roles, began its work by addressing the findings of recent projects on guidance and learner support in HE. The Employment Department funded UDACE/CNAA project on Guidance and Counselling in Higher Education had found considerable diversity of practice across the sector. Although a significant proportion of academic, specialist and non-academic staff undertook guidance and support activities, these were largely unmonitored by the institutions. There was 'a lack of overall policy for guidance and learner support, so that co-ordination and quality assurance were problematic' (Herrington and Rivis *et al.,* 1994). There were no widely accepted standards of service in operation as part of overall quality assurance procedures, so that in most cases there were no mechanisms to assure impartiality or appropriate response to demand. Modularization and the expansion of CATS activities had been accompanied by growing diversity of the student population, but without corresponding improvements in internal information and communication systems. However, the relationship between guidance and the quality of teaching and learning was beginning to be recognized, as was its important contribution to the development of systems for learner feedback.

Building in part upon this project, which recommended a development agenda broad enough to encompass the mission of all types of institution, a team from Sheffield Hallam University, supported by national advisers, concentrated on the guidance and learner support implications of an expanded, diverse, credit-based HE system, as part of the National CATS Development Project commissioned by HEQC (Robertson, 1994). One of the many recommendations of this project was that there should be a national code of practice for guidance and learner support.

From consideration of the work undertaken by these development projects, and in the context of the recently issued Student Charters, the Network identified a key priority: an expanded, more flexible, credit-based HE system must enhance the coverage, quality and standards of service delivery of its guidance and learner support arrangements.

HEQC's role, as the sector's own quality assurance body, was not to replicate project work planned by the Employment Department and other agencies, but to facilitate the development of a quality assurance and quality enhancement *framework* which any institution could use if required, and from which all could benefit if they so wished.

The Council's *Notes for the Guidance of Auditors* (HEQC, 1995b) and *Guidelines on Quality Assurance* (1994a) already offered a starting point, by drawing the attention of institutions to their arrangements for guidance and learner support which might stimulate lines of enquiry during the process of institutional quality audit. However, the *Learning from Audit* report (HEQC, 1994b) demonstrated that until recently the quality assurance of guidance and learner support arrangements has not been a major feature of audit. Institutions reported that they required a more detailed set of guidelines which were not mandatory, but which reflected the best of current and planned practice.

The development process

The challenge for the Network was to review current definitions and standards of good practice, agree a common set of underlying principles, and develop a format which was both easily understood *and* inclusive. Recent statements, reports and codifications of good practice in guidance and learner support were analysed, and from them were distilled dozens of activities and processes. These were then grouped into clusters which reflected the different *phases* of learning: pre-entry, entry and induction, on-programme and moving on. The Network was concerned that learning should not be characterized solely in terms of progression through a conventional course and so emphasized the continuity of many guidance and learner support activities throughout any piece or programme of learning, however short or discontinuous that learning might be.

Members of the Network then considered the range of guidance services and support activities as a series of *entitlements*, in different institutions and settings, and tried to match these with *responsibilities* which institutions might be expected to undertake. This provided the second organizing principle for the Guidelines. To ensure that the Guidelines could be used as a practical quality assurance and enhancement tool, the Network identified a wide range of evidence which institutions could use as an indication of whether and how well particular aspects of service delivery were being addressed.

As Sheila Cross has noted (1994), for many guidance practitioners the issue of ethical principles is even more critical than that of quality assurance mechanisms. Specialist guidance and learner support staff, such as careers advisers, managers of student services and counsellors, work to codes of practice developed by their own professional associations, and so must have regard both to the mission and policies of their institution *and* to the codes of ethics which govern their professional activity. In recent years these professional associations and other national bodies have explored common ground in a number of fora, and have set out principles on which there is broad agreement across professional groupings.

These principles provide the ethical framework for the practice of guidance and learner support. They are reflected in the Guidelines, but also in other relevant documentation, such as the Charter for Higher Education, the Guidelines for Quality Assurance, and the codes of practice of the professional bodies concerned with guidance and learner support. The principles include: learner centredness; confidentiality; impartiality; equal opportunities and accessibility. Although there are a number of other formulations, there is broad, widespread agreement about these five principles and their importance.

While many institutions would wish to subscribe to all of these principles, it is recognized that there may be conflicts of both interests and practice. For example, confidentiality is a cornerstone of the practice of counselling, financial advice and careers guidance. However, entitlements to APEL and other forms of recorded achievement may imply more open systems of transmitting information about learners. It is hoped that the Guidelines will encourage institutions to engage with these issues of principle to ensure that their practices are consistent with their stated mission and ethical stance. The network recognized the fundamental importance of institutional policies for guidance and learner support, and also included sections on policy, resources, quality and communication issues in the framework.

When the first draft of the Guidelines was complete, the document was piloted in ten institutions of different types across the country – three colleges of HE, four new universities and three older universities, including the Open University. In conducting the pilots, each institution drew together a group of staff with responsibilities for student support and guidance and considered both the principles underlying the practice of guidance and learner support, together with guidance practice in support of one or more phases of learning. This enabled institutions to achieve a variety of purposes, as well as testing the efficacy of the framework.

Several institutions were able to use aspects of the Guidelines as a basis for an audit of the scope and volume of guidance and learner support activity. Some were already engaged in the review or development of their arrangements and took the Guidelines as a starting point for discussions about change.

Feedback from this brief pilot phase indicated that the Guidelines should indicate the responsibilities of learners as well as those of the institutions, in ensuring that the guidance and support offered by the institution was used effectively. The underlying principles of guidance were reduced from nine to five, and the range of indicative evidence was sharpened.

Several heads of institutions were then asked to comment on the revised Guidelines, particularly from the perspective of compatibility with their overall mission and policies. All recognized the potential usefulness of the approach, but there were divergent views as to how far the framework should be used as a tool of internal development and how far it might be linked to the development of standards of service delivery.

As a result of the work documented above, a set of guidelines now exist which can be used by HE institutions to enhance and assure the quality of their guidance and learner support activity.

The Guidelines do make certain assumptions about HE institutions, that they:

- will wish to ensure that learners receive a range of services and support as an integral part of teaching and learning;

- recognize that learners require effective guidance and support in order to achieve their full academic potential;

- are concerned with the quality of the student experience;

- attach different degrees of importance to guidance and learner support;

- have diverse arrangements for guidance and learner support, often within one institution;

- are interested in the quality assurance and quality enhancement of their guidance and learner support arrangements;

- are developing responses to the Charters for Higher Education;

- are willing to consider the implications of the full range of guidance and learner support activities; recognize that staff roles and responsibilities for guidance and learner support are changing and may in turn require different forms of support;

- understand that guidance staff may also work within codes of practice and ethical frameworks determined by their professional bodies.

The Guidelines also assume that learners and potential learners in HE:

- are prepared to take responsibility for their own learning;

- are faced with widening choice and recurrent decisions about learning;

- are entitled to a range of guidance and learner support services;

- are willing to work cooperatively with staff and, where appropriate, their peers in achieving their own learning goals;

- are willing to offer regular feedback on the quality of their educational experience and of the guidance and support services available to them.

They also assume that institutions and learners are equally interested in both standards of service delivery and the way in which guidance and learner support can contribute to the maintenance of standards of academic attainment.

GUIDANCE AND LEARNER SUPPORT AND STANDARDS

Ever since the then Secretary of State for Education's speech of April 1994 (Patten, 1994) HEQC has been refocusing its work around the issue of standards. In terms of quality audit this has sharpened existing lines of enquiry as to how institutions satisfy themselves that their standards are being maintained and are broadly comparable with those elsewhere. In terms of Quality Enhancement, HEQC's agenda now has work on standards at the centre – and in this is included work on guidance and learner support. The rationale is two-fold: institutions, students, stakeholders and employers are interested in both standards of service delivery *and* in the role of guidance and support services in maintaining and enhancing academic standards.

If institutions wish to develop minimum, or threshold, standards for the delivery of their services to students, they should be able to do so by referring to the Guidelines to identify essential components of a guidance and learner support system appropriate to their unique mission. We know that some institutions are already using the Guidelines in this way, complementing their work on Student Charters and statements of entitlement. The idea of minimum standards for the delivery of guidance and learner support across *all* institutions has not yet won widespread support in the HE sector. However, developments elsewhere may produce changes: the recently formed National Advisory Council for Careers and Educational Guidance has undertaken a study of the feasibility of setting minimum quality standards for guidance across all sectors (Hawthorn, 1995). The imminent introduction of occupational standards and associated National Vocational Qualifications for advice, guidance, counselling and psychotherapy will also have the effect of drawing attention to the standards of service which learners might expect from both specialist and non-specialist staff in *any* educational setting (UCOSDA, 1995). The Guidelines could be adapted quite readily to provide overall benchmarks for service delivery: future work by HEQC's Quality Enhancement Group will be investigating the feasibility of this, and its acceptability to institutions.

Guidance and learner support must also play an important part in upholding academic standards. The Guidelines emphasize support for people making decisions wisely about learning at every stage. Guidance helps to ensure that learners choose programmes appropriate to their requirements, with the attendant likelihood of greater academic success. Learner support services help to ensure that learning is effective, and that the intended learning outcomes are achieved.

The integrated system of advice, support and feedback suggested by the Guidelines offers a constant source of information about learners' achievements at the point of entry to any given programme, rendering starting-points and entry standards easier to record and use as benchmarks. This is particularly important for those interested in the 'value added' by teaching and learning.

Better, more consistent guidance about the nature and outcomes of assessment is more likely to lead to more consistent approaches to assessment by both learners and teachers, in turn providing external examiners with more coherent evidence upon which to base their judgements. The development of guidance-based recording of achievement in HE also provides a parallel system of checks and balances in the assessment of student achievement.

The Guidelines are designed to cover guidance for flexible learning at all stages and in all settings. They acknowledge prior learning, off-campus learning, credit-based learning and the importance of formal and informal networks of guidance and education providers. The Open College Networks and Authorised Validating Agencies for Access Courses have demonstrated that quality assurance and the setting and maintenance of standards can be successfully undertaken by a range of agencies which share common purposes.

HEQC has evidence that the Guidelines are already proving very useful in helping institutions to identify where they want to focus their guidance quality assurance activities. For example, several institutions report that they are using the framework of the Guidelines as a checklist to 'audit' their own guidance and learner support provision. One college has modified the basic framework to include the locus of responsibility for each element of provision, the current services available, gaps in provision and further action planned to remedy them. They have, in effect, 'customized' the framework to fit their own circumstances, while adhering to the structure and key components.

Other institutions have preferred to use the framework to look at one aspect of their guidance and learner support provision, such as pre-entry guidance, or personal tutoring. Much of this work is still at the early stages, but the value of having an over-arching framework within which to consider specific aspects of provision has been emphasized.

There are concerns, however. Some institutions resent the idea of any 'bureaucratization' of what they deem to be highly individual, personal interactions. Others are resistant to initiatives from the national bodies concerned with quality, seeing the Guidelines as yet another area against which they will be audited and assessed. This was not the intention when the Guidelines approach was adopted, as HEQC's stance is predicated on institutional autonomy. However, the HEFCE has indicated that from April 1995 its assessment criteria will include student guidance and support (HEFCE, 1995). Given that it is likely that the processes of quality audit and quality assessment will be brought together within the next few years, it is not unreasonable to assume that the quality framework contained in the Guidelines may have an influence for some time to come. In the light of this, institutions, their academic staff, guidance specialists, administrators and students will need to address the issue of assuring the quality of a complex but coherent system of guidance and support in a way which does not engender highly bureaucratic, inflexible systems of monitoring and quality control.

There are still a number of central questions to be addressed:

- How far should guidance be integral to teaching and learning and how far provided by specialists? What are the implications for staff development? Should all academics aspire to achieving NVQ Level 4 in guidance once the new occupational standards for advice, guidance and counselling are established?

- Is it possible to set minimum standards for guidance and learner support services in any institution? If so, what are they?

- How far can guidance and learner support systems contribute to the setting and maintenance of *academic* standards?

- How is the quality of guidance best assured: by academic audit or by inspection or by some other mechanism?

- What impact do resource allocation patterns have on the quality of guidance and learner support, and on minimum standards of service delivery? Does better guidance always cost more?

- How can guidance feedback from learners, especially in very flexible systems, be used to enhance the quality of learning for all students, wherever they are, and at whatever stage of learning?

The Quality Enhancement Group of HEQC will be doing further work over the next year to explore some of these issues, working with a few institutions prepared to act as case studies in using the Guidelines over a longer period.

The nature of the debate about the use of Guidelines for quality assurance purposes is perhaps best illustrated by the responses of two Vice-Chancellors, heads of different types of institution. One asked:

Is there not a core of requirements which represents a minimum that should apply to any institution of higher education? (Vice-Chancellor, new university).

The other warned:

care should be taken to avoid the guidelines becoming prescriptive ...a system of universal mediocrity administered by a team of highly qualified learning support staff... the formalization of informal relationships with no evident benefit to either the student or the institution... (Vice-Chancellor, older university).

The challenge for us all is to develop a quality assurance framework which is flexible enough to cope with the vast and expanding array of HE learning opportunities, and to satisfy these rather different points of view, so that all students have the best possible learning experience, achieve their full potential and feel that they have had all their expectations amply fulfilled.

REFERENCES

Butler, L (1984) *Case Studies in Educational Guidance*, ACACE, Leicester.

Cross, S (1994) 'Guidance at the cross-roads: the case of Higher Education', paper for the Anglo-Scottish consultation on guidance for learning and work, mimeo.

Davies, G (1995) Press release, Profiles in Higher Education, January.

Department for Education (1993) *The Charter for Higher Education*, HMSO, London.

Further Education Unit (1994) *Managing the Delivery of Guidance in Colleges*, FEU, London.

Hawthorn, R (1995) *First Steps: A Quality Standards Framework for Guidance Across All Sectors*, RSA, London.

Herrington, M and Rivis, V M, with Brown, J, Jones, P and McNair, S (1994) *Guidance and Counselling in Higher Education*, HEQC, London.

Higher Education Funding Council for England (1994) *Profiles of Higher Education Institutions*, HEFCE, Bristol.

Higher Education Funding Council for England (1995) *Quality Assessors' Handbook*, HEFCE, Bristol.

Higher Education Quality Council (1994a) *Guidelines on Quality Assurance*, HEQC, London.

Higher Education Quality Council (1994b) *Learning from Audit*, HEQC, London.

Higher Education Quality Council (1995a) *A Quality Assurance Framework for Guidance and Learner Support: The Guidelines*, HEQC, London.

Higher Education Quality Council (1995b) Notes for the Guidance of Auditors, mimeo.

Imeson, R (1995) 'Students in higher education: journeys without maps', *Network News*, Edition 1, February, Guidance and Learner Autonomy Higher Education Projects, Employment Department, pp.3–5.

Moore, R (1995) *Retention Rates Research Project: Final Report*, January, Sheffield Hallam University, Division of Access and Guidance, mimeo.

Patten, J (1994) *Speech to Higher Education Funding Council Conference*, 12 April, mimeo.

Rivis, V M (1991) 'Principles and pragmatism: the development of education guidance for adults in the United Kingdom 1970–1991', University of Hull, unpublished MEd thesis.

Robertson, D (1994) *Choosing to Change: Extending Access. Mobility and Choice in Higher Education*, HEQC, London.

Universities' and Colleges' Staff Development Agency (1995) *Feasibility Study: The Application of Vocational Qualifications to Staff Development in Higher Education, Report to Employment Department*, February, Sheffield.

Watts, A G (1994) 'Journals and journeys: an interview with Tony Watts', *British Journal of Guidance and Counselling*, 22, 2, 285–96.

Watts, A G and Hawthorn, R (1992) *Careers Education and the Curriculum in Higher Education*, CRAC, Cambridge.

Chapter 2

Providing the Institutional Infrastructure to Support Flexible Learning

Lyn Oates and Les Watson

INTRODUCTION

This chapter presents a summary of the external pressures for change in styles of learning and teaching and their impact on Cheltenham and Gloucester College of Higher Education (CGCHE). Developments at the College in response to these pressures are discussed, focusing specifically on the last four years from an Information Services (IS) perspective. CGCHE is a university-sector college of 7,000 students, of whom 5,200 are full-time. The College has undergraduate and taught postgraduate accreditation; research degrees are awarded by the University of Bristol. Around 80 per cent of undergraduates follow a modular degree course.

There are four faculties within the institution. The Faculties of Arts and Education, Business and Social Studies, and Environment and Leisure are teaching faculties. The fourth, the Faculty of Information Services, provides essential support services for both staff and students, covering administrative computing, academic computing, library, flexible learning development and delivery, reprographics, design services, AV support, photocopying, networking and telephones.

FORCES FOR CHANGE

In common with most HE institutions, the issue of efficiency has been high on the agenda for some time, with reductions in the 'costs' of teaching (and learning) of central concern. Quality issues have also gained influence as institutions seek to enhance the entire student learning experience (CTISS, 1991) and especially their learning environment. The force-field diagram shown in Figure 2.1 gives a summary of some of the perceived forces promoting and inhibiting change at CGCHE and other institutions.

16

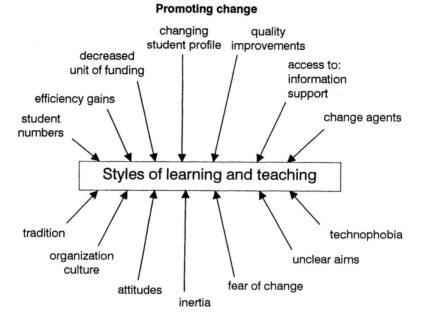

Figure 2.1 *Forces promoting and inhibiting change in styles of learning and teaching*

The difficulty of promoting changes in learning and teaching styles is increased as student numbers increase and funding per student decreases, putting pressure on academic staff time and the unit of resource available. For many institutions the negative resourcing aspects have been offset by significant financial assistance for learning and teaching innovation from such funds as the Teaching and Learning Technology Programme. At CGCHE, changes in learning and teaching have been promoted largely from within existing resources with some input from Enterprise in Higher Education (EHE).

Putting learning first

There has been a considerable amount of work by staff in higher education which has produced a range of flexible learning materials, both paper-based and on computers. However we believe that the widespread adoption of flexible approaches to learning cannot take place in HE without the development of appropriate institutional infrastructure. If flexible, student-centred approaches to learning are to be embedded in an institution, then robust support structures, and a culture that encourages change, need to be put in place. The Faculty of Information Services at CGCHE aims to provide a sound resource base on which the culture change can be built. The building of an appropriate resource base provides a foundation for learning development. It will then be possible to construct College policies on a wide range of issues such as finance and estates which put learning before teaching and verify the changed culture for the College community.

The role of information technology

The importance of information technology in promoting changing styles of learning and teaching is acknowledged at CGCHE and IT resource provision forms an important part of the strategy. The model shown in Figure 2.2 of learning developments supported by IT is a modified version of the ICL/MIT 1990s model of business development with IT observed in many successful companies. It is not a recipe for achieving success with the use of IT in learning but is a descriptive model which summarizes current and possible future IT developments in support of student centred learning at CGCHE.

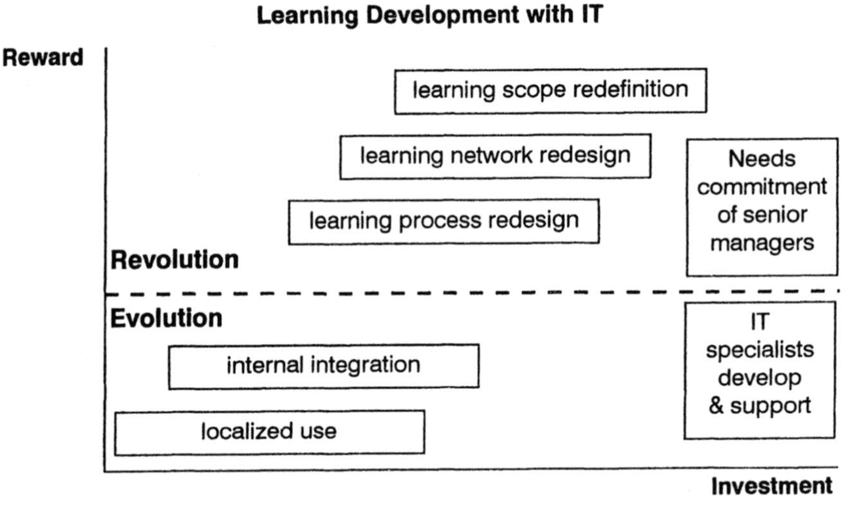

Learning Development with IT

Reward

learning scope redefinition

learning network redesign

learning process redesign

Needs commitment of senior managers

Revolution

- -

Evolution

IT specialists develop & support

internal integration

localized use

Investment

Figure 2.2   *Based on the ICL/MIT 1990s model of business development with IT (after Margaret Bell, NCET Chief Executive, Resource conference, November 1993)*

This graph highlights the fundamental importance of the involvement and commitment of senior managers. If IT is to lead to the learning revolution that is widely expected, senior managers have to be involved and support that revolutionary phase of development shown in Figure 2.2. Although the importance of IT as a tool for learners has been acknowledged by many practitioners in HE, there is so far little hard evidence that education generally, and HE in particular, has succeeded in fully exploiting the potential of current IT systems for learning and teaching. As Professor Bob Lewis states (CTISS, 1991):

Little research has been undertaken on the uses of IT to support learning in HE... when compared with other learners undergraduates do not feature much in any literature concerned with IT.

What the computer brings to the independent learner is the ability to edit, that is change their work. Being able to edit with a computer is an obvious, but powerful, feature which is taken for granted. We believe that editing is the fundamental key to the power of IT as a tool for learning. Editing a piece of text, modifying a graphic image, or developing a computer program, involves making changes, thinking these through and solving the problem. Thinking through and solving problems is a sound basis for successful independent learning. Consequently IT is an essential foundation stone in any flexible learning infrastructure.

DEVELOPMENTS AT CGCHE

The strategy adopted at CGCHE to develop institutional support for learning and teaching contains five distinct but equally essential components, all of which are vital for success. Many of the following changes have taken place in parallel over the last four years:

- integration of traditional library, IT and AV support services at the managerial and operational levels;

- development of an appropriate IT infrastructure;

- development of a cooperative working relationship between the College Professional Development Unit, Enterprise in Higher Education, and Information Services;

- establishment of a Flexible Learning Development Unit;

- formation of a College Teaching, Learning and Assessment Committee.

Integration of Information Services

The first stage in service integration was the establishment of Learning Support Services in 1990. This integrated library, support for academic information technology, and AV support at the managerial level, was primarily for reasons of cost efficiency. As the learning and teaching debate gathered momentum it was realized that there were potential gains to the institution of the merged service developing a more proactive role in the support of learning and teaching. The institutional decision in 1992 to rename Learning Support Services as Information Services and promote it to faculty status was an important signal to the staff within the service and those working elsewhere in the College, indicating that the developing role of Information Services had the full support of the senior management. Since then the Faculty of Information Services has emerged as a change agent moving the focus from an emphasis on teaching as the primary activity of the institution, towards learning. The Faculty of Information Services, having no major investment in teaching, is an obvious candidate to promote such change across the College. It is now the mission of IS to:

- be customer responsive;

- develop strategies for further integration of services;

- be proactive in learning and teaching developments.

Learning centres

In the summer 1993, computing and library resources were physically integrated in refurbished accommodation and learning centres were established for combined delivery of traditional library and IT services.

These centres are now in the process of further development and IS aims to evaluate the use of space and resources to promote and encourage student-centred approaches to learning. Student and lecturer evaluations obtained through quality assurance procedures, course committees and customer perception surveys inform developments. Changes to the learning centre environment aim to encourage and facilitate students who wish to take a more active role in their learning. At CGCHE it has been recognized that learning centres should provide a place where all students can work using a range of learning styles and resources, individually or in groups and independently at their own pace and level.

Current efforts focus on developing an easily accessible information-rich learning resource and aim to ensure the continued promotion of independent and flexible approaches to learning. For example, a flexible learning area was created in the spring of 1994 to provide a focus for all learning support resources and thus provide an integrated learning environment for the student at an operational level. Located within the main College learning centre, this area is now a centre for independent learning, access to learning resources and utilization of information resources. Study spaces are equipped with networked computers alongside other learning resources. Flexible learning area staff have a range of skills in information and its associated technologies and participate in the training programme mentioned below. The following resources are available in this area:

- networked CD-ROM facilities;

- access to JANet;

- on-line access to over 500 remote databases;

- flexible learning resources including both print-based and computer-based learning materials;

- a staff development collection of materials to assist both the in-house development of flexible learning materials and purchase of commercially produced materials;

- open learning centre for study skills support and tutoring;

- language laboratory.

In recognition of the changing role of IS staff as facilitators, there has been considerable investment in staff development and training. IS closes for one hour per week to provide training time for all IS staff to ensure that they develop the necessary skills to respond to the changing information needs of lecturers and students. This is in addition to an investment of the equivalent of 2 per cent of payroll to funding other IS staff development activities.

Information technology developments

At formation in 1990, the College had a small number of IT-literate staff and a range of incompatible and somewhat outdated IT equipment. In order to develop an IT culture appropriate for a learning organization, an IT strategy was produced which aimed to provide individuals with the tools and skills required to become productive knowledge workers. Key parts of the IT strategy were to:

- *develop a College network*: over the last three years a College network has been installed linking staff on all sites.

- *provide machines for academic staff*: at the same time a programme of providing a computer for each member of academic staff has taken place. The machines are supplied connected to the network and have a package of integrated software covering word-processing, spreadsheets, presentations and e-mail.

- *provide IT training*: a range of IT training courses are provided which cover the use of the hardware and the software package supplied to staff. These courses are provided free to all staff.

Links with other College units

The close working relationship developed between Enterprise in Higher Education, the College Professional Development Unit (PDU) and IS has been an important enabling factor in the developments at the College. These three units have been at the forefront in recognizing the need for change through cooperation. They each have an individual and unique focus which, combined, have generated a positive impetus for change. This cooperation has ensured that the resources of EHE could be linked to the developmental role of the PDU and the implementation role of IS to ensure that projects produce viable products.

Enterprise in Higher Education (EHE)

The College was successful in 1990 in obtaining EHE funds of £1 million over five years. This funding has played an important role in College-wide flexible learning developments. Initial work in this area by EHE was on an individual basis. Members of the College were able to bid into EHE funds for financial support to develop learning and teaching materials, but this proved to have disappointing results and produced little in the way of widely applicable learning resources.

More recently, cooperation between IS and EHE resulted in a successful bid for substantial funds to set up a Flexible Learning Development Unit with the role of coordinating and stimulating cross-College learning and teaching developments (see below).

Professional Development Unit (PDU)

The College Professional Development Unit was established at an early stage in the life of the College, with a brief to address learning and teaching issues across the institution. An important outcome of the close working with IS was the production of an institutional audit of teaching, learning and assessment. This was carried out to provide a snapshot of the situation in May 1993 and to contribute to the College strategic plan which stated:

> The aim of the College is to create an innovative, enterprising and accessible high quality learning environment that enables individuals to develop intellectual, scholarly, creative, problem solving and decision making skills (Freeman and Thorne, 1994).

Not surprisingly, the audit showed that much of the teaching of the institution was of a very traditional nature and based largely around lectures making little use of new technology. The purpose of obtaining the 1993 snapshot was to provide a point from which to monitor developments in learning and teaching and also to provide a discussion point for learning and teaching issues.

Flexible Learning Development Unit (FLDU)

This unit was established with the support of joint College and EHE funding in 1994 to provide central support for the development of learning materials. This is achieved through project management in the construction of learning materials in' conjunction with the provision of editorial, courseware design and production expertise. Funds are available to second members of academic staff to the FLDU to provide the appropriate knowledge base for the production of learning materials. During the last eight months, 12 projects have been started, several of which are being piloted for student evaluation in Autumn 1994.

The unit also aims to influence learning methodologies within the institution through the encouragement of innovative learning developments and by taking a proactive role in multimedia developments. The unit is currently engaged on a project in partnership with the PDU to design and deliver a staff development programme to promote new learning technologies.

The FLDU also works closely with staff in the flexible learning area to ensure appropriate support of student-centred learning delivery.

Teaching, Learning and Assessment Committee

A Teaching, Learning and Assessment Committee was formed in 1994 as a sub-committee of the College Academic Board which aims to coordinate the increased activity across the College as members of staff seek the most academically-appropriate as well as most resource-efficient methods of delivering the curriculum and assessing students.

Its role includes the consideration of learning and teaching issues in general, the coordination of flexible and open learning initiatives, policy development, and dissemination of good practice both inside and outside the institution.

SUMMARY AND CONCLUSION

The strategies outlined above represent a package containing elements which address the need for an infrastructure capable of supporting current and future changes in learning and teaching. This emphasizes the importance of a shared understanding of the need for change addressing both material and human resource issues. Staff development and the collective action of internal change agents (IS, PDU and EHE) are seen as vital in the promotion of learning.

There is now a firm foundation for future learning and teaching developments within the College. Institutional commitment to independent and flexible learning at the strategic level and the newly formed Teaching, Learning and Assessment Committee will encourage a new phase of College-wide cooperation. The Faculty of Information Services is committed to the provision of positive support for independent learners alongside access for all to an information-rich environment.

REFERENCES

Computers in Teaching Initiative and Support Service (CTISS) (1991) File 11 'Computers in higher education teaching and learning: some aspects of research and development', March.

Freeman, R and Thorne, M (1994) 'First steps towards the virtual university', University of Sunderland, International Symposium for Independent and Flexible Learning.

Mason O'Connor, K and Watson, L (1993) *Audit of Teaching, Learning and Assessment*, Cheltenham and Gloucester College of Higher Education.

Chapter 3

Towards Total Quality Education: Policy and Implementation of the Students' Charter

Michael Gregory

BACKGROUND TO THE CHARTER

The Charter policy initiative was introduced by the British government in 1991 and was intended to raise the quality of services by organizations in the public sector. The Charters for Education (National Charter Frameworks have been written for both further and higher education) were introduced in September 1993. They deal with the rights of students and the local community (including employers) in the provision and delivery of education by universities and colleges, although some organizations (for example local authorities) are also referred to in the Charters.

The political agenda underlying the Charter includes a number of priorities:

- reducing the cost of educational investment;
- improving choice, widening of services and offering redress for the individual consumer of public services;
- providing increased value for money through wider inspection and benchmarking of performance;
- placing an emphasis on diversity of provision through innovation and flexibility within the framework of competitive advantage, providing greater motivation for local delivery of improved services.

Each Charter sets out a framework for standards of service which can be expected by the consumers of educational processes. The aim is to ensure a developmental approach to the way in which educational institutions deliver their business.

The Charter for Higher Education (CfHE) refers to the quality assurance roles of both the HEFCE (Higher Education Funding Council for England), responsible for the actual quality of education provided, and the Higher Education Quality Council (HEQC), which is the body responsible for checking that institutions have satisfactory quality assurance systems for controlling the quality of their educational provision. The Further Education Funding Council (FEFC) has gone one stage further than the HEFCE, however, and has indicated that colleges in the future will not only be enjoined to produce their own Charter specifying local standards, but that individual college levels of performance against them will form part of FEFC inspections, including whether 'all members of staff are aware of and respond to the commitments in [both] the National Charter... and the college's own Charter' (FEFC, 1993).

A FOCUS ON THE CUSTOMER

The Charters for Education form part of the Citizens' Charter initiative launched by the Prime Minister in 1991 (Command 1599, 1991) as a major aspect of government policy. The aim was intended to raise the quality of delivery by public sector service providers through improving the standards of information and openness, choice and consultation, courtesy and helpfulness, putting things right, value for money, and independent validation. Deakin (1994) has argued that beneath the Charter philosophy lie layers of New Right political theory:

> the concept of political choice, with its dire warnings of the inherent self-interest of public bureaucracies and perpetual risk of producer-domination; and the importance of transforming the character of transactions between state and citizen so that they come to resemble more closely those that take place in the market (pp.48–9).

The Student Charters need to be placed not only within the wider context of the Citizens' Charter initiative, however, but within the framework of government policy as a whole which is concerned with the range of public policy initiatives to ensure that government money is not only spent economically, efficiently and logically, but also to secure a maximum return on investment.

The Student Charters follow others: citizens', parents', the National Health Service, for example, and reflect a focus on a 'customer-led' notion of education. However, this aspiration brings a host of difficulties. Using the language of 'the customer' means that HE bodies need to be defined as 'service organizations', characterized by Hill and Taylor (1991) through:

> the extent to which the customer is involved in the delivery process itself; the potentially more variable nature of the delivered service, compared with a manufactured product; [and] the impermanence of the quality of the service (p.6).

As a service industry, education and training is positioned in an extraordinarily complex market situation. The customers of educational services are not only individual learners but also (in the case of younger people) their parents, employers, sponsors and sometimes Local Education Authorities (LEAs) or Training and Enterprise Councils (TECs). Additionally, many providers of educational services need to rely on income generated by consultancy to corporate clients and research commissioned by contractors (see Guy, 1991). Each of these client groups has a range of priorities, interests and needs, and their requirements may, in fact, conflict. Previously lacking a determined notion of who the customer was, therefore, it is easy to see how universities and colleges as providers of learning often embarked on a route which was perceived by the end of the 1980s as far too provider-centred.

Similarly, the notion of identifying what is actually sold as a 'good' or 'service' in education is just as complex. Often, the direct consumer of what is offered by the provider is not the one paying for it, and the former may, as a beneficiary of educational services, have very different aspirations from the purchaser. Educational provision is also nebulous and difficult to define in 'retail' terms. Each customer is generally buying his or her own individual package of learning, with unique and personal expectations from it. This complexity is also compounded by the sophisticated components which make up the educational product that is sold, and which not only includes a curriculum composed of learning and assessment, but access to a range of other support and entitlements beyond this curriculum.

There is also the need to 'educate' the perceived market itself that there is a market. The notion of 'empowering' customers through rights embodied in a Charter presumes a sophistication which may not be there yet, or which at most may have, on the one hand, vocal interest groups which might take advantage of other, less powerful or more naive corpora. This may be particularly true in the university sector, where the prevailing paradigm in many institutions has often been centred on the premise that the university was its own custodian of what is good and right, and where the 'customer's' involvement has often been kept at distance by closed doors beyond which the concealed mechanisms of university processes actually function.

THE AIMS AND OBJECTIVES OF THE NATIONAL CHARTER

Many of the provisions of the Charters, which are qualitatively rather than quantitatively inclined, are already in place in colleges. Few numerical targets are mentioned and the provisions of the Charter are given in the form of what students and employers have 'a right to expect'. Some are of a fairly general nature.

The Charter for Further Education (CfFE) is structured around the rights of users in respect of:

- information about further education services and individual colleges including exam results and student destinations;

- equal opportunity issues;

- guidance and admission arrangements including grants and fees;

- the quality of the course and learning programme and facilities available;

- information about what to do if anything goes wrong.

Similarly, the CfHE centres on the above, and particularly around:

- information about the institution and its services;

- performance of institutions in the sector;

- accommodation and facilities;

- financial support and welfare;

- procedure for entry;

- the role of the students' union.

Essentially, the Charters set out a framework for the standards of service that customers can expect. In designing them, account was taken by the Minister of State for Further and Higher Education of the National Union of Students' (NUS) own Charter, which saw the role of a students' charter as

> providing the underpinning for a quality education system [which could only] be achieved by making students central to [the] vision of what Further and Higher Education is and should be (NUS, 1992).

The Charters therefore encompass the notions of:

- empowerment of the student to choose, direct and control his/her education;

- the idea of citizenship of an educational community;

- a quality system responsive to the needs of students.

In essence, the Charters are codes of practice designed to ensure levels of customer satisfaction, a process which itself has been described as continuous and 'which does not begin or end with a purchase; it covers the entire "ownership experience" from selecting a product, to purchase, through aftercare to repeat purchase' (Smith, 1994). In educational terms, this equates to the learner career notion of pre-entry, entry, on programme and exit: that is, from information being available about what services are available, to information about what is on offer, to guidance and counselling about choices, to delivery of curriculum and learner support, and beyond to how the student uses what is learned after progression into further learning or work.

THE IMPLICATIONS OF IMPLEMENTING A LOCAL CHARTER

Suffolk College is a complex organization, with over 34,000 individual students. In its five-year strategic plan, the College indicates a Total Quality Management (TQM) aspiration (Suffolk College, 1994). The College has also made a commitment to achieve Investors in People accreditation, and there is a view that the Student Charter will provide, within a TQM approach, the means for making more explicit the standards which reflect defined or stated needs of service users, providing what Pollitt (1990) has described as an emphasis on:

> the central importance of service user (or consumer) judgements of the appropriateness and effectiveness of services... [a] demystifying... basis for a more intelligible system of public accountability... [and which includes]... the actual experiences of those processed (p.437).

Employing almost 1,000 full- and part-time staff, the institution has network arrangements with a range of organizations, including complicated validation and franchise agreements with partner providers. These dispositions have to be considered when implementing any local Charter, which itself needs to take account of a number of factors in the design process:

- Should a 'mixed economy' institution have a single Charter covering both further and higher education provision, including common redress procedures?

- What account should be taken of students on franchised courses?

- How can the Charter be designed so that it can facilitate a clear statement and procedure for student satisfaction?

- How can the Charter be used to ensure quality?

- What steps can be taken to ensure that the Charter itself does not set a 'lowest common denominator' standard?

- What are the costs involved, and can the institution afford the provisions in the Charter?

- How can success against the Charter be measured?

- What sanctions might be available if Charter provisions are not met?

- Can the college produce the required information and services?

- What staff development is necessary to ensure that all staff are aware of the Charter and of their responsibilities in its implementation?

- To what extent is the college organized to undertake valid surveys of customer opinion, and how will the results of such surveys be published?

- Is there a learner agreement in use by the college and does it set out the student's agreed study programme and the college's and student's responsibilities to each other?

- How speedily will the college be able to respond to complaints, and will the college's complaints procedure be published?

- How will the Charter be used to achieve competitive advantage?

A resulting aim of any TQM approach is to create a learning organization, with 'a focus on good internal communications, and well integrated training and development focused on business goals and strategy' (Holloway, 1994).

The Charter itself, while giving benchmarks against which to evaluate performance, is only one strand of a strategy aimed at organizational improvement. In the department of which the author is Dean, a two-point approach is being taken to take the Charter beyond rhetoric to a real tool for business development. At the same time as a monitoring group is being formed to look at all aspects of the department's systems and performance against each Charter objective, the Investors in People (IiP) accreditation is being worked towards. IiP is a business development tool, with a focus on customer service through clear planning, with communication to, involvement by and development of all employees. It is a process approach which can underpin the product and service aims of the Charter aspirations.

SYSTEMS AND COLLEGE PROCEDURES RELEVANT TO CHARTERS

The Charters are aimed at locating the development of quality standards within a culture of continuous quality improvement for post-compulsory education generally, and with an expectation that each college will develop its own strategy and infrastructure for quality, delivering a truly national service that is locally provided (Boswell, 1994).

In recent years, most colleges, including Suffolk College, have developed quality procedures, many elements of which can be incorporated into a college Charter. These include: quality management systems; marketing, promotional and public relations materials and activities; student handbooks and prospectuses; equal opportunities policies; health and safety procedures; student services; learner agreements/contracts; and curriculum entitlement/mission statements/corporate statements of purpose.

Some of these documents, however, may not be sufficient to entirely meet Charter requirements, and must be carefully examined to ensure that they are not geared just to younger full-time students, but encompass the growing market of continuing education students, as well as corporate clients. Similarly, in many cases, procedures and policies have often been drawn up without student consultation, and may need revision in the light of this requirement. Current policies and procedures will also need to be backed up by specific service standards, and will require a mechanism for enforcement and redress. Finally, any existing procedures need to set both improvement targets and a means of incorporating customer feedback, customer views being seen as central and crucial user judgement about the appropriateness and effectiveness of the services provided.

CHARTERS – THE ENTITLEMENT/PARTNERSHIP DICHOTOMY

Some universities, as well as all colleges, now have Charters. One of the significant debates encountered by the majority of institutions when designing them has been the dilemma whether a student Charter should be an agreement giving guaranteed levels of service between the institution and the consumer, or one that invokes a spirit of partnership between supplier and user, stating what each party might expect of the other.

An examination of the John Moores University Charter indicates six pledges to students: to facilitate access and operate a fair and efficient admissions procedure; to publish full and accurate information about the university's activities, procedures and regulations; to provide a suitable learning environment; to give a suitable student support network; to involve students in its decision-making processes and to operate a fair and efficient complaints procedure. In return, students are expected to display responsible attitudes towards staff and fellow students; to comply with the university's regulations; to study diligently; to respond to reasonable requests from staff; to take advantage of extra-curricular opportunities and in addition to participate in the university's decision-making processes.

The issue was also faced by Sheffield Hallam University. This institution has made substantial progress with a document detailing the levels of service students can expect on general issues, the curriculum and on central services, in effect dissecting the university's product into levels of service provision which have items such as accommodation or catering at the simple end and teaching and learning at the other end of a continuum of complexity.

Huddersfield Technical College has, in its notes of guidance to staff on the college's student Charter, spelled out the nature of the approach to be one of partnership: 'the charter is an attempt to let students and staff know exactly where they stand in relation to student rights *and* (emphasis added) responsibilities' (Huddersfield, 1994).

Suffolk College, in constructing its own Charter, has adopted the 'creed of partnership', believing a Charter can only be successful if it reflects a genuine partnership with students which is based on trust and accompanied by a clear understanding of responsibilities and entitlements.

PUTTING A CHARTER IN PLACE

All colleges by now will have addressed the process of mapping their own policies and procedures against the requirements of the national Charter, and will have produced a local version. In implementing a Charter, however, institutions will need to address some significant political issues, and may well be prompted into a radical rethink, not only of their own philosophical approach to quality, but also a review of their current policies and procedures in light of the Charter's place in the life of the institution.

In deciding on how the Charter will be implemented, colleges will not only have to decide what can be afforded (and quality does not come cheap) but also the extent of these financial costs to students. Institutions will also need to address how the qualitative indicators are to be measured; and of significance in the entitlement debate is the notion of sanction and remedy, or redress for unsatisfactory services. The NUS has argued on this last point (1993) that financial compensation is not the most appropriate remedy when something goes wrong, and that it is more important to ensure speedy redress and correction. The legalistic (quasi) framework is of major interest in this area. A Charter has been defined as:

> a statement of rights, or rights and responsibilities, between an institution and a group of students: an 'agreed statement' or one imposed by government or by institutions (Davey, 1992).

While this is different from a contract, nevertheless it is important to examine if a Charter can give rise to legally enforceable obligations. The complexity of this issue is compounded by being intertwined with the legal nature of the university or college itself, and what has been termed as the peculiar dichotomy of its public-private character (Lewis, 1983), that is at one level, creating rights and obligations contained within a public law framework; and within a different frame, a relationship of a private nature between the provider and its customers giving rise to enforcement through civil law remedies.

Farrington (1994) points out that whether or not Charters will have any legal effect 'will depend upon the extent to which they are expressly or by implication terms of any contract between the student and the institution' (p.320). There is little doubt that a college has a contractual obligation to teach to a syllabus which is part of a course and which has, through its publication by the institution, encouraged a student to enrol (D'Mello v Loughborough College of Technology). Furthermore, there is a common law obligation to teach it to a 'reasonably professional standard' (Sammy v Birkbeck College).

Student concern about teaching and assessment broadly falls into two categories: first, dissatisfaction with the decisions (usually of assessment) which the institution has made. Here, normally following an exhaustion of the college's or university's internal appeal system, the student would have potential remedies in public law, bringing into play natural justice principles, for example, if they had been breached, or judicial review if any maladministration had occurred (although there maybe some limitations on this in the university sector by virtue of the 'university visitor' system which operates essentially by Royal prerogative).

A real uncertainty, however, is how far contractual principles offer a potential avenue for redress when an institution fails to live up to its commitments. For example, one of the clauses in Suffolk College's Charter indicates that the student can expect: 'support for your learning including high quality teaching'.

There is at least an implicit suggestion that the terms of the local Charter in this case are to be incorporated into the contract between a student and the college. The expression of a right to 'high quality teaching' seems to indicate a standard beyond what might be a 'reasonably professional standard' (of which 'satisfactory' might be the lowest common denominator), thus imposing a greater obligation on the institution, as well as widening the scope for potential litigation by a 'consumer' who feels he/she has received less than a 'high' standard of teaching.

TOTAL QUALITY MANAGEMENT OR TOTAL QUALITY EDUCATION?

The charter policy has been criticized as 'opportunist consumer rhetoric' (*THES*, 1993) and as indicated above, there are serious obstacles (particularly in universities) at a systemic level as well as at a behavioural level in gaining acceptance to the notion of a customer-led focus on educational delivery. The other problem with the Charters is that colleges will only pay service to them. They were introduced to colleges and universities as part of government policy, with no real consultation. This was at a time when newly-independent colleges were beginning to find some firmer anchors following the acquisition of corporate status. Ironically, it is this independence, which many see as a 'divide and conquer' strategy for the further education sector, which led to little, if any, resistance by colleges about the way in which the Charters were introduced. While commitment to a local Charter from the top of an organization might well start to initiate a culture change, the resistance to 'yet another initiative', particularly where there is a belief that Charters in other sectors do not appear to be working, should not be underestimated.

For those institutions which do see the student Charters as a means to begin to implement a total quality approach however, the opportunities are there to gain competitive advantage over others in a market becoming incrementally more competitive. Total quality, though, demands a completely different corporate attitude involving everyone in the quality process, where detail is important, a sustained commitment is needed, and where the continued maintenance of standards is an imperative. It entails an extensive investment in people through training and staff development and clear understandings of quality levels and ownership of problems, combined with a commitment to change and improvement, as well as a sharing of responsibilities and burdens through participation.

The student Charter is here. For colleges in the further education sector, funding depends on performance measured against it. In universities, it is a means of differentiating and protecting provision in a mass higher education market.

The real objective, of course, is that the rhetoric of TQM, ISO/BS Standards, IiP, and other kitemarks do not take over the reality of the need to ensure that what is necessary is total quality *education*, in effect an approach based on the development of education and training provision which is founded upon an holistic approach to quality, relevance, responsiveness and accessibility.

REFERENCES

Boswell, T (1994) 'Speech to the Conference', by the Parliamentary Under Secretary of State for Further and Higher Education, at the Annual Conference of the Further Education Funding Council, 10 February.

The Citizens' Charter (1991) Command paper 1599, HMSO, London.

Davey, B (1992) 'The Student Charter Project Report', University of Kent.

Deakin, N (1994) 'Accentuating the apostrophe: the Citizen's Charter', *Policy Studies*, 15, 3, 48–58.

DfE (1993a) *The Charter for Further Education*, Department for Education, London.

DfE (1993b) *The Charter for Higher Education*, Department for Education, London.

D'Mello v Loughborough College of Technology, The Times Law Report, (H C 17 June 1970).

Farrington, D J (1994) *The Law of Higher Education*, Butterworths, Oxford.

FEFC (1993) *Assessing Achievement*, Further Education Funding Council, Circular 93/28, HMSO, London.

Guy, R (1991) 'Serving the needs of industry', in Raggatt, P and Unwin, L (eds) *Change and Intervention: Vocational education and training*, Falmer Press, London.

Hill, F M and Taylor, A (1991) 'Total Quality Management in higher education', *International Journal of Educational Management*, 5, 5, 4–9.

Holloway, D G (1994) 'Total Quality Management, the learning organisation and post-compulsory education', *The Vocational Aspect of Education*, 46, 2, 14–28.

Lewis, C B (1983) 'The legal nature of a university and the student-university relationship', *Ottawa Law Review*, 15, 249–73.

National Union of Students (1992) *Student's Charter*, NUS.

National Union of Students (1993) *The Right to Learner Agreements*, NUS.

Pollitt, C (1990) 'Doing business in the temple? Managers and quality assurance in the public services', *Public Administration*, 68, 435–52.

Sammy v Birkbeck College, The Times Law Report, (H C 3 November 1964).

Smith, I (1994) *Meeting Customer Needs*, Butterworth-Heinemann, Oxford.

Suffolk College (1994) *Strategic Plan, 1994*, 9, Suffolk College Corporation.

THES (1993) 'A Student's charter'. Leader comment in the *Times Higher Educational Supplement*, 8 November, p.12.

Chapter 4

What Price Reflection?

Robert Simpson and Tony Wailey

INTRODUCTION

Within the context of the changing nature of student demands and the call for greater accountability of the quality of the service HE offers, this chapter proposes a model for the delivery of student learning development entitlement in HE set within a framework of academic guidance. AP(E)L practice is used principally to credit learning but in the current context it will be used to play a more significant role in the diagnosis of the nature of the students' total learning experience. In order to achieve this, we propose a wider interpretation of the function of AP(E)L, with more emphasis on assessment and less on accreditation, a clear analysis of learning development and a three-phase application of the interrelationship between AP(E)L and learning development for entry, on-programme and exit of a student's time within a programme of study. In this way, it becomes a mechanism for the effective delivery of a student's entitlement through the integration of guidance and learning development support. In addition, we examine key areas of concern that HEIs are increasingly being asked to address in order to achieve a more coherent and systematic delivery of students' English language development entitlement.

BACKGROUND

All of us working in the HE sector are acutely conscious of the pressure to provide a quality service for our students in the context of increasing numbers and decreasing resources. The scrutiny of quality comes in a variety of guises. Principally, we are meeting it through the quality assurance mechanisms now vested in HEFCE (Higher Education Funding Council for England) and HEQC (Higher Education Quality Council) and the 1990s phenomenon of Charterism that has spawned the DfE, HE and the NUS (National Union of Students) versions and countless individual university charters (*pace* the previous chapter).

At the University of East London (UEL), our mission statement is not untypical in its commitment 'to provide the highest possible quality of education' and 'to encourage the participation of the local community'. At the same time the institution is committed to 'widening access for mature, non-traditionally qualified and ethnic minority students'. In practical terms, the widening of access means that there is a growing number of students with increasingly diverse backgrounds and expectations. Some of the typical characteristics can be identified as:

- long absence from education;

- mixed previous educational experience;

- a breadth of experience;

- unpreparedness for HE;

- unfamiliarity with UK system and academic conventions;

- linguistic diversity;

- lack of clarity about what is required;

- early anxieties;

- lack of confidence;

- increasing outside commitments/pressures on time management.

At UEL we are familiar with the statistics: (45+ per cent over 25, 54 per cent ethnic minority, 60+ per cent mature students), but what are the implications for improving the overall quality of the learning environment to achieve higher participation and attainment levels? The answer to this question rests with our ability to resolve the dilemma of meeting the learning needs of students within a mass system by anticipating and predicting their portfolios of need and ensuring the development of their learning skills.

This rapidly evolving situation carries implications not just for the content of the curriculum, but also for its delivery, especially with reference to the learning development needs of our students. The Charters concentrate on standards of service relating to aspects of learner support, that is the totality of the services that students can expect, but are less forthcoming when it comes to learning and teaching. The Further Education Unit (FEU) in its 1993a document, *Supporting Learning – Promoting equity and participation*, defines the notion of learning entitlement: 'All learners are entitled to a range of learning opportunities which will enable them to fulfil their learning goals and ambitions and improve their life chances'.

Given the changing profile of students, many HE institutions must analyse very carefully how this is delivered in practical terms for their students' benefit. The student profile within a mass system has changed and how its needs are met requires rethinking. In particular, HE can no longer assume that all students bring with them the requisite skills to participate in and succeed. HE is having to pay more attention to the learning development needs of students. The FEU document quoted above draws attention to the learning development needs of *all* our students and also introduces the notion of additional support targeted at specific 'at risk' students. Some learners require specific, additional support to help them meet these goals and to allow them to participate and achieve fully.

Learning development entitlement therefore, recognizes that students are entitled to develop their learning at any level in the mainstream curriculum. Learning development systems support any student who needs to develop skills to cope with a level of study. It defines the student's learning needs from the situation of the student, the overall development of a student's learning skills, the demands of a learning programme, the levels of study, the demands of assessment and the teaching methods used. It is important to note that it is not only concerned with improving an individual's skills, but also with reviewing the demands imposed by the organization on the curriculum and the methods of teaching. The responsibility does not rest entirely with the student either in the case of claiming for experiential learning to be accredited or in proving suitability to join a programme of study. If we recognize, as UEL does, that learning takes place everywhere, the trick is in the attempt to assess or measure the integrative process.

Figure 4.1 is adapted from the Taxonomy of College Services in the FEU document, *Learner Support Services in Further Education* (1993b). It separates out the learner services, column A, from learning resources, column C. The key focus of this chapter is the central column, column B, the actual delivery of learning development, for it is proposing a model for the delivery of aspects of learning development entitlement in HE which is set within a framework of academic guidance. In this way we feel that the personal tutor system, which has traditionally been the vehicle for addressing individual learning needs and which has come under stress to the point of collapse, can be given a clearer role and fresh purpose. The different elements listed in column B receive priority during each of the three stages of a student's academic life, ie (pre)-entry, on-programme and at exit.

There is a degree of overlap between the terms used in column B, for example progress reviews and recording achievement, because we have included the widest range of terms currently being used. This also raises the issue of when assessment begins, continues and ends as seen from different points on an individual's learning curve. The different elements of delivery detailed in column B arrive from a number of developments. These include those advanced by the Enterprise in Higher Education Initiative which has highlighted the needs of the autonomous learner with particular reference to the requirements of the labour market but more significantly, many which have been integral to students' learning experience before they entered HE. However, the principal influence has been the collaborative work of staff involved in promoting a learning development model within the University of East London and staff responsible for the embedding of AP(E)L practices. Two projects in particular helped to formulate the proposed model.

Learner services	Learning development	Learning resources

Student services
Counselling
Health/welfare
Catering
Childcare
Accommodation
O/S student care
Financial services
Access funds
Recreational
Registry
Careers
Student Union
	Entry
	ROAs
	Guided admissions
	Induction
	Initial assessment
	AP(E)L
	Assessment and
	   accreditation
	Additional support
	   assessment
	
	On programme
	Tutorial support
	Personal/professional
	   development
	Recording achievement
	Profiling
	Action planning
	Concurrent experiential
	   learning
	Progress reviews
	Careers education unit
	Core skills
	Transferable skills
	Learning development
	   safety net
	Additional support
	RBL support
	Subject-specific
	   curriculum
	   workshops
	
	Exit
	Exit guidance
	Progression counselling
	Transfer documentation/
	   transcripts
	ROAs
		Library services
		Learning centres
		Open learning facilities
		Study centres
		Computer networks
		IT facilities
		Multimedia technology
		Learning packages
		Audio-visual aids

Figure 4.1 *Learning development framework*

One of those projects was an ESF (European Social Fund) funded programme, APL for Refugees. Although this was a short intensive AP(E)L programme principally aimed at accrediting the prior experience and qualifications of mature students gained outside the British education system, it was immediately clear that the curriculum had to address learning development and, in particular, language development issues before any articulation could be made in using credit systems. The other project involved work at another level where we were developing a model for personal and professional development (PPD) within a recently SEDA-validated Certificate in Teaching and Learning in Higher Education, in which it has been found that AP(E)L is not particularly applicable unless attributed to the core modules of the programme. The PPD unit acts as the spine to the programme. It asks new lecturers to identify what they know already and to carry out a needs-analysis while also taking 'snapshots' of their development on programme/at work and concluding with a reflective exercise in which they wrap up their experiences of the programme, but not their personal and professional development. The programme ends, but their professional profile is ongoing throughout their professional lives.

Both instances raised questions about when assessment ends and when accreditation takes place. In one instance we were dealing at level O (pre-entry level) and in another at level M (postgraduate). More importantly, we were using the same methodology, the difference being the level of learning outcomes expected from the respective cohorts of participants. The question was how to integrate the methodology used in these two projects and how it could be applied at levels 1, 2 and 3 within the undergraduate degree scheme (UDS). In short, where would this methodology interact with the totality of the student's learning experience and importantly, how would it demonstrate the way in which guidance and learning development is managed within the whole institution? This is pertinent when considering the impact of modularization and the growing recognition that programmes of study have to go beyond the internal coherence of each subject module or unit. What became increasingly clear through working with two cohorts at such opposing levels was that AP(E)L and learning development models could usefully serve each other's different but mutual ends to implement such key aspects as diagnosis, action planning, the recording of progress and tracking of students.

ASSESSMENT OF PRIOR EXPERIENTIAL LEARNING – AP(E)L

Many candidates for assessment of academic credit towards a qualification claim both certificated and uncertificated learning and for them the process begins with the academic evaluation of their certificated learning, moving onto assessment of their uncertificated or experiential learning.

General credit is that which may be awarded to a student for activities which are recognized as being of academic value at the appropriate level. The credit recognized does not relate to any course on which the student is registered but is an academic judgement expressed in credits on the achievement of prior learning. Specific credit is that which may be awarded towards the attainment of a specific programme of study. This is any type of general credit which is seen as being sufficiently relevant to count towards the award for which the student is registered.

In practice, because of quality judgements, there is considerable debate between the apportioning of general credit to specific credit. This raises the issue of portability of credit between institutions and the culture of specific programmes. More importantly, as Boud *et al.* (1993) point out, this raises questions about the relationship between assessment and accreditation:

> We cannot tell in advance what knowledge we will make our own ... learning from experience is often far more indirect than we pretend it to be. It is not a simple, rational process.

Many definitions of AP(E)L concern themselves principally with accreditation without noting that these are assessment processes in the first instant. If we look at the purpose of assessment in learning development, we find that the diagnosis of need is primary and linked to the assessment demands of a particular programme of study. So AP(E)L and learning development meet at the primary focus on assessment as seen in the development of a student's learning skills in relation to the demands of a learning programme and the integration of this process into particular levels of study. Within a learning development framework, AP(E)L raises the question of where assessment/diagnosis of need begins, continues and ends as seen from different perspectives of an individual's learning curve.

Viewed in this manner, AP(E)L and learning development share similar purposes in assessment rather than accreditation. In many instances AP(E)L is only brought into operation as an extension of an admissions procedure. As in the case of learning development, it should also have a preparatory, monitoring, supportive and evaluative function throughout a student's time within HE. This aligns AP(E)L much closer to the guidance, mentoring and monitoring roles as outlined in the Robertson Report (1994) and SEEC (1994–) projects in the establishment of credit frameworks.

AP(E)L should not only be carried over into the curriculum but should be concerned with how personal constructs of experience and learning can be credited mid-way through a programme of study, for example, how concurrent experiential learning is to be supported. This in itself would illustrate the number of ways in which learning and epistomological issues could be articulated, besides assisting students to note their own learning processes as well as the multi-interpretative paradigms which characterize learning in HE. AP(E)L is central to this process given its context within the framework of learning development (see Figure 4.1).

The AP(E)L model in practice

The AP(E)L process within this context of pre(entry), on-programme and exit assessment involves four exercises and can operate at any level. The exercises are a position paper (personal profile with needs analysis), an extended cv based upon a specific taxonomy of learning achievement, documented past and present learning outcomes, and a critical review, a reflective learning exercise.

At the end of this process is a planning/exit exercise, with an opportunity to analyse and reflect upon performance. Students, irrespective of the time spent on such an exercise, provide a completed portfolio, including all the products above. The portfolio provides a crucial point of reference for the monitoring of an individual's learning development, for establishing learning goals and strategies for their realization as well as for articulating the processes of critical reflection, credit and assessment that accords with a structured self-development programme at any level. The exercises are illustrated in more detail below.

1.   The self as central to the learning process: a position paper based on where the participants are coming from, where they are now, where they hope to arrive and how they are going to achieve this. In many ways, an abbreviated version of a Learning Contract associated with a humanist cognitive perspective.

Example of a Personal Profile

After the decimation of the motor trade and the huge redundancies which followed, in 1967 I moved to London and worked on London Transport as a Station Foreman. I left London Transport in 1969 to work as an Insurance Agent for a large company...

I moved back to London... in 1975 and took a job as manager of a restaurant with an international company. The company was just moving into the British market and I moved on to be Director of Operations and Development responsible for expanding the restaurant chain. This involved doing a large variety of jobs including finding locations, negotiating the property deals and working with the architects on refurbishment.

In 1979 I became involved in housing issues and with other tenants formed a pressure group to fight for better housing conditions. This developed into a full time paid job as field worker cum general secretary for a federation of tenants organization. This caused me to become politically involved with all housing sectors. In that capacity I sat on many committees.... My interest was developing practical policy into policy practice and encouraging new and innovative ideas about housing management with the emphasis on changing the power relationships between management and tenant. I developed a particular interest in the concepts of accountability through structure and communication with the emphasis on positive rather than negative accountability. This was not a timely activity as the Establishment was moving in exactly the opposite direction.

It became clear after ten years that this was a lost cause in the current political environment and I resigned in 1989 to care for our 1-year-old child so that my partner could return to teaching. I have spent the past four-and-a-half years as a full-time father and second-rate house-husband.

I have gained more from my childcare experience than from any other job I have done.

Such an exercise encourages students to begin the process of contextualizing their own learning experiences specifically within the academic environment. This position paper model can be extended to allow students to make a claim for credit and more importantly to outline and assess what their past learning involved. It is in this context that the self is central to the learning process.

2.   The second asks students to analyse by means of an extended cv what skills, knowledge and personal qualities they possess in relation to their work experience. This is based on taxonomies of skills and knowledge and focused very much on behaviourist philosophy of trying to identify systematic educational objectives which include affective learning (Carter, 1985).

Example of an extended CV

EMPLOYMENT
1980–1985 Private Music Teacher/Recorder Player

Job Description
As a private teacher I offered lessons in recorder playing to children of all ages and adults. This involved preparing pupils for exams, competitions and performances.... Working with a group performing 14th–17th century music on copies of original instruments.

Personal Qualities
The ability to interact with a varied client base (from 4-year-old prodigy to middle-aged executive looking for a new hobby). Personal motivation to work without college's support. 'Salesmanship' to attract students and performance jobs.

Skills
Organization of time, personal curriculums, concerts and festivals. Cooperation with parents. Evaluating an individual's needs and negotiating with them a set of targets. Personal musical skills of performance.

Knowledge
Technical knowledge of the instrument and playing techniques. Knowledge of both teaching and performance repertoire. Knowledge of requirements of exams.

This exercise indicates a progression from the personal profile to a more analytical framework with which students can demonstrate different forms of their learning. It is the sequencing of that learning that benefits students approaching the rigour demanded by peer assessment, seminar papers, written assignments and those learning skills that HE demands of its students, regardless of level.

3.   A switch in focus takes students to a third assignment which is based more on a social constructivist approach to learning to describe the outcomes of specific work situations (Kolb, 1984). This model needs to be more prescriptive before the participants start to use assessment to negotiate their own learning situations.

Study/work-based learning outcomes

Refer to David Kolb's Learning Cycle. You could also use this framework if you wished to incorporate any short courses you have undertaken and would want to include within your portfolio:

Experience	Job which requires something of you.
Reflection	The special situation you find yourself in. The context which relates to the problem you encountered within your experience above.
Conceptualization	Problems encountered (list them from above) and can the student identify these problems in a different way?
Evaluation	What learning has come from this cycle? We would demonstrate this as learning outcomes.

You could then structure your study/work-based learning into:

(a)   a description of the job/programme
(b)   the specific situation of yourself to the job/learning programme
(c)   the problems you encountered and attempt to structure and re-structure
(d)   the learning outcomes that arise from 'evaluating' all of the above links in the cycle.

For anyone engaged in the assessment of prior learning, the difficulties of identifying learning outcomes with the learner at the centre, the categorizing of knowledge, skills and personal qualities, the different attributes of extracting learning from experience in precise statements, are all well categorized.

4.   By the end of the AP(E)L process, the student will have engaged with relevant prior learning, assessment and needs analysis of knowledge, skills and personal qualities, the integration of the learning outcomes from past and present experiences of study and work and the whole process of assessment issues concerning personal development. The overall analysis of this process of the student's learning will be finalized in the form of a 1,500-word narrative, the critical review, based upon the concept of the 'reflective practitioner'. The critical review calls on students to reflect on

and assess the process of the component parts of their programme of study. It characterizes the different attributes of the programme and how the student engages with them to produce a final, summative evaluation. Such an evaluation can also serve as a synoptic planner for further development.

Implementation of the Model

Figure 4.2 sets out the possible components of the delivery of learning development, second column, and the AP(E)L process, third column. The AP(E)L column represents the four separate products a student produces which go towards a final portfolio as described in the previous section. They correspond with the three key phases of a student's HE career: (pre-)entry, on-programme and exit, column four. The first column refers to the different skills that receive priority during the three key phases. The threshold skills are those identified by the programme as the ones needed initially by a student to gain entry to a programme of study. The core skills are those that a student will need to participate fully and which will be addressed principally in the first year. By the end of the programme the student will have developed a set of transferable skills that are expected of a graduate. The second column indicates some of the practical ways in which the learning development needs of students can be realized. These are the various elements which would help give a renewed function to the current personal tutor system which is struggling to stay alive, by switching towards an academic guidance focus with more clearly defined activities and end results.

Skills	Realizations	AP(E)L product	Phase
Threshold	ROAs Skills audit/diagnosis Action planning Learning agreement	1. Position paper 2. Extended CV	(Pre-) entry
Core	 Profiling Learning outcomes	3. Work-based learning outcomes 4. Critical review and	On-programme

Transferable	Additional support
	Careers/education
	   unit
	Monitoring and
	   tracking
	
	ROAs
	Progression
	   counselling
	Transcripts
		portfolio	Exit

Figure 6.2 *Higher education learning development*

Such a model has advantages not only for the student but also the institution and can help achieve a higher quality of a student's total experience:

Student benefits
- provides an academic guidance framework in the absence of personal tutors
- links up with students' pre-HE experience
- guarantees early diagnosis
- focuses on goals and strategies to achieve them via an action plan
- helps measure own progress
- gives greater control over own learning
- can draw on continued support throughout HE career
- helps realization that learning is for life, ie postgraduation
- addresses students' changing priorities as they progress through HE
- increases understanding of the processes of learning
- helps develop analytical skills and demands of programme of study and HE
- starts this process on familiar ground, ie self.

Institution benefits
- acts as a spinal organizational mechanism to promote coherence
- runs through a student's entire stay in HE
- reduces the dangers of fragmentation that modularization can bring
- safeguards a standardized approach yet is adaptable to subject specific needs
- can be validated and accredited
- sets concrete tasks with clearly defined end products
- guarantees early assessment of individual student learning needs
- promotes critical thinking and powers of analysis through reflection
- encourages course teams to analyse the learning development needs of students
- encourages course teams to analyse the learning development demands of their programmes
- complements educational practice in other sectors
- links services which support the learner from pre-entry to exit guidance and beyond into lifelong learning
- improves participation, retention and completion rates.

Implications for English language development entitlement

The proposed framework can be tested out against one specific area of learning development, that of English language. This does not just concern overseas students but also speakers of other languages and English as a mother tongue. The present day HE student profile means that individuals will have varying degrees of competence and performance in the standard English required in the formal academic HE context. The difficulties students encounter with their English are too often viewed from a deficit model position which sees student needs in terms of deficiencies in ability, previous education, suitability for a programme and standards, and consequently refers to additional learning support as remedial provision. The proposed framework defines the student's development needs from the situation of the student, the overall development of a student's learning skills with an analysis of the demands of a learning programme, the levels of study, the teaching methods used and the demands of assessment. In this way, learning development is placed firmly within an *entitlement model* and it is not only concerned with improving students' skills, but also with reviewing the demands imposed by the organization on the curriculum and the methods of teaching.

Integral to this more positive focus is the assessment of English language threshold levels, which is crucial to establishing effective language development systems. This would be placed within an admissions system that is part of an institutional advice and guidance framework, one of the chief recommendations of the Robertson Report, that is, redeployment of resources to ensure better quality educational guidance. The English language development needs of a student would be part of the assessment of the learning development needs that would operate within such a framework of academic guidance, with a structured assessment of prior learning, recognition of existing evidence students possess, and the drawing up of an action plan based on an assessment of and mechanisms for the monitoring and tracking of a student's progress. The framework emphazises that the function of assessment is not simply to credit learning but also to diagnose needs. This diagnosis is seen in terms of the individual student's learning requirements but equally important is the assessment of the demands of the chosen programme of study. Subject area teams analyse their programmes in terms of the English language demands of their programmes, in particular the minimum threshold level required.

Testing is not the only means of assessing appropriate English language threshold levels. Students bring with them evidence in a variety of forms: ROAs, GNVQ core units, GCSE/A-level English/Communications qualifications, A/S General Studies, LOCF levels and completion of Access courses. Such evidence is only useful if set against work done by subject areas to analyse the level of English language demanded to gain admission, participate on-programme and successfully complete. Despite such guidelines which indicate acceptable/recommended minimum levels/qualifications and equivalences, there will be a number of students who can provide no acceptable English language threshold level evidence. This is an at risk category. Systematic assessment of student language enables such students to be identified at an early stage who can then benefit from the additional support that is provided within the framework. Equally, there is no point accepting students who do not have the necessary language skills to benefit from studying, even if they were to receive additional support.

The experiences of those students from the projects detailed earlier suggest that, from vastly different perspectives and levels of attainment, they have benefited from the methodology laid out in the model. Although only a small sample, when added to the evidence provided by both AP(E)L and learning development case studies in individual UEL faculties, there does seem scope for the introduction of such a model to the Undergraduate Degree Scheme (UDS) at levels 1, 2 and 3. How to bridge the price of reflection for the individual within the mass system, between pedagogic and financial constraints, between the equitable and the economic, is the central question.

CONCLUSION

The 1993 NUS Charter highlights funding as a key issue:

> one of the main problems in Higher Education at present is underfunding... one area where underfunding is increasingly becoming a problem is student support services. In many, though not all, institutions funding for student services has failed to keep pace with the increasing numbers of students. Further, many of the non-traditional students entering Higher Education are likely to use such support services more intensely. Adequately funded support services are integral to the quality of education.

Practitioners know that in today's world, new models are largely achieved through the pump-priming of external funding sources such as the European Social Fund, SRB and so on and other European sources along with inventive use of existing baseline and cost recovery funds.

To implement the model proposed in this chapter is a pointless exercise unless backed up by base-line funding. The traditional approach based on enrolment ('bums on seats'), has in the past encouraged the formulation of strategic and operational plans centred around the subject curriculum. However, the changes in funding methodology towards a target-led enrolment base balanced by the key factors of retention, completion and output-related funding creates a possible space within this hegemony for learning development entitlement. Educationalists need to use this space, this opportunity, to develop entitlement and rationalize the shift by putting forward resource arguments. Exploiting this space makes financial sense as it protects the investments of the resource managers, the students.

We argue for an all-through model of learning development incorporating the best practices of AP(E)L, adaptable to the changing priorities of the different phases of a student's life in HE. HE should recognize that learning development is not a peripheral concern but core provision, and that adjustments need to be made to work towards policies that place the student at the heart of provision. This has the advantage of meeting the demands of government Charters and quality assessments which are placing greater priority on learning development issues.

Crucially it makes sound economic sense. To ignore the issues is short-sighted for institutions relying on high retention rates and high degrees of success in order to reach expected target funding. This model helps ensure students are recruited on the appropriate programmes, that they are assessed and inducted, that they stay and succeed. Students stand to benefit and we, as educationalists, can feel confident that we are involved in quality provision.

REFERENCES

Boud, D, Cohen, R and Walker, D (eds) (1993) *Using Experience for Learning*, SRHE, Guildford.

Carter, R (1985) 'A taxonomy of objectives for professional education', *Studies in Higher Education*, 10, 2.

The Further Education Unit (1993a) *Supporting Learning – Promoting Equity and Participation*, Staples Printers, Kettering.

The Further Education Unit (1993b) *Learner Support Services in Further Education*, Blackmore Press, Dorset.

Kolb, D (1984) *Experiential Learning*, Prentice Hall, Englewood Cliffs, NJ.

Robertson, D (1994) *Choosing to Change*, HEQC, London.

South East England Consortium (SEEC) for Credit and Transfer (1994-) *Towards a Regional Credit Framework*, Forthcoming, 1996.

Chapter 5

Student Guidance on Modular Schemes: The Need for Integrated Systems

Jan Bamford and John Goodfellow

INTRODUCTION

> Discharging students unguided into a morass of learning opportunities is
> likely to produce an alienation and dislocation from the productive bene-
> fits of learning which may be just as constraining to the fulfilment of
> learning potential as former arrangements may have been (HEQC, 1994,
> p.264).

This quotation from a recent Higher Education Quality Council report suc-
cinctly highlights the consequences of the inadequate provision of student
guidance to support greater student choice. Regrettably, the burgeoning move-
ment supporting greater flexibility and student choice pays scant attention to
the issue of student guidance and, where positive signals are found, there is
evidence that they should be treated with caution:

> Universities and colleges are generally well-disposed towards the principles
> of educational guidance but this is not reflected in either the resources or
> the status awarded to the activity (HEQC, 1994, p.267).

One explanation for this was also identified in the same report which stated that:

> institutional strategies have tended to emphasise the advantages that
> modularisation bestows upon the management control system rather than
> for the expression of student choice and mobility (HEQC, 1994,
> pp.236–8).

In practice, the pressure on resourcing student guidance provision may be even
greater, as the extent to which efficiency gains are achievable in credit-based
modular schemes is debatable and the limited evidence available is mixed
(Robertson, 1992; Watson, 1989).

Institutions wishing to introduce greater student choice with integrity need to recognize that additional costs in the provision of student guidance will be inevitable. It is argued that the level, type and timing of student guidance required in modular schemes will primarily be a function of the nature of the scheme and of the student population. This will be a natural consequence of developments if, as the National Institute of Adult Continuing Education anticipates:

> Learning programmes will normally be individually constructed from a range of modules, designed to be coherent in the terms of the individual's own needs and the necessary disciplines of the subjects studied and the requirements of professional practice (NIACE, 1993).

As individual learning programmes replace traditional course structures significant economies of scale in the provision of student guidance will be lost. Historically academic coherence has been a guiding principle in the design of courses and has therefore been created at a collective rather than an individual level. Providing guidance to support students creating their own individually coherent programmes is therefore an additional cost of increasing student choice.

Furthermore, an integral component of traditional courses is an established network of standardized procedures, regulations and communication devices which provide staff and students with a widely known and accessible knowledge base. Both these formal systems together with informal networks of values, expectations and norms form the basis of the course culture which, in many cases, provides a significant support mechanism for students sharing similar experiences and problems. It is therefore clear that management needs to recognize that the numerous benefits offered by greater student choice and flexibility are accompanied by demands for new types of student guidance and the loss of guidance systems associated with traditional courses.

We attempt here to identify and discuss key issues determining the type, level and form of student guidance on modular schemes. This is followed by a critical analysis of one support system which has been designed as an integral part of the infrastructure for a business modular scheme with which we are involved. Experience with this scheme, including positive feedback from students, has lent support to the view that student guidance is most appropriately located close to students' learning experience and that the structure and processes of any student guidance system should be a function of the nature of the modular scheme and of the characteristics of the students. We further argue that an integrated approach is required in the design of student guidance support systems for modular schemes. Guidance can be viewed along a continuum which commences at the scheme design stage, where significant 'empowering' and 'constraining' decisions are made, and progresses to embrace support for students' scheme/subject selection and programme construction, 'in-programme' guidance, through to exit guidance.

In contrast to recent HEQC proposals which recommend the development of a dedicated professional para-academic service, we argue that guidance should be brought close to the student's main programme experience and provided jointly with personal tutorial support.

Through an analysis of the relationship between course structures and requisite student guidance systems, we suggest that management must accept that the benefits offered by modular schemes, in terms of greater student choice and flexibility, carry with them higher student guidance costs in comparison with traditional courses where significant economies of scale are achievable. Student guidance costs can be reduced by providing comprehensive on-line module databases, standardizing pre-entry or early-entry programme planning forums, and by utilizing students as mentors.

FACTORS DETERMINING THE TYPE AND LEVEL OF STUDENT GUIDANCE

We contend that the level and type of student guidance required is primarily determined by the nature of the scheme of study and the characteristics of the student body. It is therefore imperative that the scheme design stage is used to identify and define the composition of student guidance systems.

Two factors are central to the required level of student guidance within schemes. The first of these is the level of intra-scheme and inter-scheme choice. The level of intra-scheme choice will be a function of the number of options available to students on their main subject/field of study and the number of subjects/fields within their main scheme. The level of inter-scheme choice is primarily determined by the number of 'free' modules students are entitled to select. At the University of North London free modules (ie, modules available from any undergraduate scheme within the University) constitute one quarter of a student's programme. As the level of choice available to students outside their main or home field/subject increases, the problems of providing student guidance become more complex and the need for institution-wide systems of support becomes greater.

The degree of intra- and inter-scheme choice is also determined by the number of levels of study and the nature and frequency of prerequisites and co-requisites. Traditionally, undergraduate courses have three levels of study, corresponding to the three years of full-time study. Greater freedom of choice is available within modular schemes which have only two levels of study, preliminary and advanced, where the distinction between the second and third years of full-time study are removed. Prerequisites and co-requisites are key constraining influences and their specification is a function of the culture of the organization and of individual subject disciplines. Thus at the University of North London, the specification of prerequisites is more demanding in the science and business faculties than in the social science and humanities faculties.

The second key factor influencing the demand for guidance is the characteristics and circumstances of the student population. Traditionally the undergraduate population of universities has been dominated by school and college leavers with relatively independent lifestyles, subject to varying levels of parental financial support, studying on a full-time basis. The needs of this group contrasts markedly with those of the growing number of mature students who frequently bring with them financial, domestic and other commitments and responsibilities which influence and constrain their ability to study. Changes in the circumstances of such students have implications for their studies and may require modifications to their programme of studies. Mature students, studying on a part-time basis, are more likely to need guidance in response to changes in their circumstances.

A key role of student guidance is in deciphering and demystifying the myriad of scheme regulations and documents, thereby empowering students to make more informed and meaningful choices and progress. The reality of most schemes is that actual choice is significantly more restrictive than students are led to believe. Two common examples of this are in relation to credit transfer and timetabling. Applicants are frequently led to believe that their 'transfer value' is measured in credit points obtained from their initial scheme of study. The reality is that general credit points represent only a negotiable form of currency which may range from full to zero value in exchange depending on the relationship between the source and the target programmes of study. The availability of modules is also subject to timetabling constraints which restrict the ability of students to select modules, due to timetable clashes or inter-site travel. Indeed the recent HEQC report uses strong language to describe the situation: 'Scheduling is regarded as a "nightmare" in the United States and it appears to be little different in the United Kingdom' (HEQC, 1994, p.254). Universities are currently developing strategies to alleviate such constraints by the use of central timetabling and by offering modules in both semesters and on different occasions within the week. It should be remembered that both options tend to reduce economies of scale which are potentially available from modular schemes.

It is widely recognized that the degree of choice available to students during the latter stages of their programmes is significantly influenced by the modules studied at earlier stages. It is important that this is recognized at the scheme design stage and an appropriate strategy developed. One approach is to specify a common core programme for ranges of fields/subjects within a scheme. In some business schemes, the core programme covers the whole of preliminary level studies, although more commonly it applies to a smaller proportion. The rationale for such an approach is that restricting choice, normally by reducing students' ability to construct narrow specialist programmes, at the formative stages of programme planning can result in wider choice in the latter stages of programmes. It is imperative that where choice is available, from the outset a high level of programme planning guidance is available to students during the formative stages of their programme construction.

THE CONTINUUM OF STUDENT GUIDANCE: A CRITICAL ANALYSIS OF THE METHODS UTILIZED ON ONE BUSINESS MODULAR SCHEME

This section critically examines the effectiveness of a student guidance system designed to support students undertaking programmes within a business modular scheme at the University of North London. At present the scheme is restricted to five joint undergraduate subjects, 'half degrees', which can lead to ten joint honours awards. The 'half degrees' are also available to students wishing to construct a joint programme with a 'half degree' from another faculty. However, students studying on inter-faculty programmes are supported by a different support system and administrative infrastructure. Plans are currently in progress to subsume the existing Combined Business Scheme (COMBOS) within a faculty-wide Business School Undergraduate Modular Scheme which will also embrace and extend the existing portfolio of single honours courses.

COMBOS students are required to compile programmes comprising eight modules at each of the three levels of study equivalent to the three years of a full-time honours degree. At all three levels, they are obliged to select at least three modules, including those specified as compulsory, from each of their two chosen joint subjects. Two 'free' modules (ie, modules available from their two subjects or any undergraduate scheme within the University) may be selected at each level subject to the normal prerequisite constraints. 'Free' modules therefore constitute 25 per cent of programmes.

In the design of the scheme, special consideration was given to the level, type and timing of the support that would be available to students. Experience within the Business School had demonstrated that the traditional personal tutorial system operated most effectively when feedback and counselling on academic progress was provided in conjunction with first level pastoral care. It was also recognized that the complex modular structure of the Combined Business Scheme placed major programme planning demands on students and that this required additional support. In view of these two considerations, a new joint role of Programme Planning and Personal Tutor (POPPET) was created. For the first cohort of students it was also agreed that we, the scheme coordinator and the admissions tutor, would act as POPPETS. The academic members of the scheme are assisted by a scheme administrator who also has administrative responsibilities for a range of courses.

Pre-entry guidance

The provision of information and advice for potential applicants is an essential function within the admissions process. Such guidance includes information on entry requirements to the institution, accreditation of prior experience and learning, modes of study available, options for choice on a potential scheme of study, in addition to more traditional information about the institution and the support services available. For modular-based schemes of study, a catalogue of modules within (or in addition to) the traditional prospectus would appear to be the most appropriate and efficient source of information for potential applicants prior to institutions making offers for programmes of study. This method is supported by HEQC.

Experience has demonstrated two essential problems with pre-entry guidance. First, information that is available at the pre-offer stage is often complex and while it is readily comprehensible to the experienced academic, it is frequently confusing to applicants with limited knowledge of modular schemes and the language of academics. Second, the experience of many universities is that only a small proportion of applicants actually enrol; the ratio of applicants to places on COMBOS is 15:1. In order to improve the cost-effectiveness of the recruitment process, open days are used as a means of providing guidance to groups of applicants, although individual guidance is available on request. Our experience is that existing students provide an extremely effective resource base, which is highly valued by applicants during open days. All applicants with non-standard qualifications and experience meriting consideration, together with a small proportion of 'standard' applicants, are interviewed.

Once an unconditional offer of a place on a scheme has been accepted by an applicant, a new and more programme-focused stage in the guidance process commences with provision of detailed information in a comprehensive 50-page student handbook for the scheme. However, the utility of programme planning information and other guidance sent to and provided for applicants at the post-offer stage depends critically on the time of the offer and the motivation of the student. Applicants receiving offers during September have little time to assimilate the mass of information they receive and practical issues (such as securing accommodation and grants) frequently take priority over academic issues. For those schemes of study which do not have recourse to UCAS clearing and which interview a high proportion of applicants, pre-entry guidance tends to be more effective. This contrasts with our experience where over 800 pre-clearing applications and approximately 400 September applications are received for less than 100 places, the majority of students being recruited during the first two weeks of September.

Induction guidance

In common with induction programmes at most institutions, our induction programme provides the newly enrolled student with information on the learning opportunities available to them, the first level of support available within the structure of the scheme and the variety of centrally provided support systems, such as learning support, financial advice, counselling and careers advice. It is at the induction stage that academic guidance begins in earnest, as this is the first occasion on which many of the students would have had the opportunity and inclination to study the nature of the scheme in any depth.

The induction programme we offer takes place one week before the commencement of the first semester and attempts to clarify, as far as possible at this early stage, students' initial queries and concerns and to introduce the variety of programme choice available on the scheme. Prior to induction, most students would have identified little more than their joint honours subjects. Further academic guidance is then offered during the induction programme by means of a dedicated programme planning workshop. This takes place once students have had an opportunity to consider the available learning choices for their programmes in written format and after an initial briefing session. The workshop is convened by the academic member of staff who has been allocated to a specific group of students, that is, their POPPET. An initial assessment of students' programme needs and educational requirements is carried out. Existing students are also utilized during the workshop session to act as mentors for the new students.

As part of the induction programme, students may obtain additional module information for the study of modules outside the Business School by accessing an on-line University database which offers the module availability, the level of study and a brief description of all the modules that may be studied at the University.

A student's initial programme, (in written format) for the duration of their studies is agreed with the tutor then entered on the computerized student record database. Students are required to produce a programme for the duration of their studies, as this forces them to think ahead to ensure that they understand the consequences of their choices in the formative stage of their programmes.

During the induction programme, students are also introduced to the scheme administrator who will provide their primary point of contact for many routine factors such as timetabling queries and messages for staff, for the duration of their studies. It may be argued that the comprehensive induction programme is a resource-intensive process both administratively and academically. However, high levels of staff involvement in the short term produce significant long-term benefits to students. First, an academic is able to offer guidance at the outset for a scheme which has only one common compulsory module. Second, early queries and confusion will be identified and resolved before uncertainty leads to anxiety and lack of confidence in the scheme. Third, the newly enrolled student will feel reassured at meeting their POPPET prior to a potentially confusing and chaotic first few weeks. The diversity of our students' backgrounds, circumstances and entry points mitigates against the ability to provide standardized systems of guidance and dictates the necessity for guidance to be provided on an individual basis in many cases.

In-programme guidance

Guidance on the modification of programmes of study should be available to every student at all stages of their programmes of study. This should include guidance on changing individual modules, subjects/pathways or institution. In the 1994 HEQC Report, reference is made to institutions identifying the educational guidance function as an essential part of learning, ranking alongside the provision of libraries and learning resources. This type of guidance is achieved on the Combined Business Degree Scheme during the programme through formal and informal contact arrangements with students and their POPPETS.

Immediately after the induction programme, students' individual programmes of study are considered in order to evaluate their academic coherence. Individual tutorials are then arranged early in the first semester to assess the programme of study and the possible career and learning needs of each individual student. The student's programme is therefore effectively negotiated with his/her POPPET taking into consideration their academic strengths and aspirations. This is an ongoing process during the student's stay in the University which, we argue, should be conducted alongside the tutor's pastoral role, as this enables the most accurate assessment of the students' learning needs in the light of their academic performance and personal circumstances.

POPPETS are therefore regarded as an essential point of contact by students. Students identify that their POPPET will be able to offer more than administrative advice and a reliant and confidential relationship will develop. The emphasis on the reliance for all types of guidance by the students cannot be over stressed on a large and complex modular programme of study. Feedback from students indicates that the lack of a traditional course cohesion of such a programme develops a need for identity with a central point of contact. The faculty further developed this structure by ensuring that the tutor for the one compulsory module, business skills, would also be their POPPET, thus providing a weekly focal point of contact for students. Although this is a part of formal teaching, informal feedback from students demonstrates that they find this contact reassuring and that it furthers the developing relationship. It has also aided the development of an EHE pilot profile on student competence that the University set up during the first year of the scheme. As the POPPET is also the business skills tutor in the first semester of students' programmes, a skills portfolio may be developed and monitored as students progress through their programme of study.

This is obviously a resource-intensive exercise but management must recognize the benefits of this system when a greater choice and flexibility is offered to students on such a scheme of study. Another problem that could be identified at the outset of such a system is that it is person-dependent, in that each POPPET would have considerable personal knowledge about each of their tutees. Some sort of centrally-located record system is needed and this again requires administrative support in addition to academic support. Interdepartmental study should not be seen as a hindrance to tutors' ability to offer advice, as suggested by HEQC. Within the University of North London, such programmes of study are dealt with by a special interfaculty office. POPPETS therefore deal with programmes of study of students studying exclusively within the Business School.

Formal meetings take place once a semester to give feedback on the academic progress of the student and to identify possible changes needed in a programme of study. Guidance is given on the students' academic requirements as suited to their development. Informal arrangements for meetings follow the personal tutorial model of weekly office hours for students. These sessions are often taken up, with programme guidance, especially in the early stages of the semester. It is argued by the HEQC that such in-course guidance could be given by a para-academic service dedicated to the provision of guidance and support, as personal tutors may lack the information to give cross-departmental advice and are subject to restrictions, as a result of resource allocation, on the dedicated time available to each student. However, this would not offer the familiar relationship that guidance based on the personal tutorial system offers. Comprehensive administrative support is provided in addition to this academic support through faculty administrators and the scheme administrator, who together provide a constant point of contact and reference for students.

During the course of their studies it is important for students to be provided with career guidance. This should be given by a professional service offering such opportunities as employer visits, recruitment events, monitoring and feedback arrangements. HEQC considers that this separate service is something that should be available for students to access and should not be combined with educational guidance. Institutions, given the example of successful career advice services, should invest the same resources in educational guidance as have been invested in career advice in the past.

This scheme of study has not reached the stage of an exit year at UNL. It is appreciated that professional career guidance should be reserved for the specialist department offering such a service in any institution. However, it should be noted that a consideration of the nature of programme advice has to be the students' motives for a programme of study. This is particularly true of the business field. In the subject of marketing for example, a student may wish some initial career advice before approaching the career service at exit stage of their programme of study. Such advice on their choice of marketing modules in their programme of study may be given by the student's POPPET. Once again, the POPPET is the natural point of contact for such advice. A central administrative service which dealt with cross-faculty programmes of study would not be in the position of offering the same advice as well as a specialist in the academic field who knew the student well.

CONCLUSIONS

It is self-evident that the benefits of extending student choice through modularity will only be effectively achieved if students are able to make informed decisions. The provision of student guidance should therefore be an essential component of any modular scheme and, all other things being equal, will be more resource-intensive than that required for traditional courses of a similar size. The critical issue for modular scheme planners is therefore the type, level and form of support provided.

This chapter has argued that the primary determinants of these issues are the level of choice available to students, the characteristics of the student population and the nature and duration of programmes of study. Thus it is imperative that student guidance should be considered as an integral component in the design of modular scheme systems and infrastructures. Implicit in the concept of freedom of choice is the freedom of students to make mistakes and the role of student guidance is to ensure that students' understand their responsibility and to assist them in undertaking informed choices.

We argue that student advice is most effectively located close to the student's main learning experience (that is, the main subject they are studying) rather than at a specialist but remote university-wide department. However, responsibility for the construction, coordination and updating of information databases on module availability is most effectively located centrally within an institution.

The roles of academic and non-academic support are complementary but different. The primary role of non-academic support is in the provision of information appertaining to student records, module information, timetabling, and general administrative issues of concern to students. Such support is often available on demand because of the higher level of accessibility of non-academic staff. Academic advice serves different purposes in terms of assisting students to interpret and utilize information provided by the system and in assessing the implications of students' initial choices, feedback on academic performance and changes in personal circumstances on their future programmes of study.

Experience within the Business School at the University of North London has demonstrated that student guidance is provided more effectively when general academic and basic pastoral advice is provided jointly by one tutor and that, where possible, the student's initial tutor should remain with students throughout the duration of their studies. Evidence includes feedback from students who comment favourably on their ability to build a relationship with a member of staff who they identify with their learning experiences. The nature of the relationship provides students with the reassurance to seek and obtain guidance in an environment in which confidentiality is assured.

REFERENCES

HEQC (1994) *Choosing to Change: Extending access choice and mobility in higher education,* HEQC, London.

NIACE (1993) *An Adult Higher Education: A vision – a policy discussion paper,* National Institute of Adult Continuing Education, London.

Robertson, D (1992) 'Courses. Qualification and the empowerment of learners' in IPPR *Higher Education: Expansion and Reform.*

Watson, D (1989) *Managing the Modular Course,* SRHE/OUP, Buckingham.

Chapter 6

The Unitized Wheel of Fortune

Annette Wilson and Stephen Wilson

INTRODUCTION

The BSc (Hons) Computer Studies Degree Scheme at the University of Portsmouth consists of four named degree pathways spanning the disciplines of science, business and humanities, and involving staff from three of the five university faculties. The scheme is unitized, allowing students the opportunity to choose, within some limited constraints of their degree pathway, from over 100 units across the three disciplines.

During the first year, students study compulsory units spanning the whole scheme. With this breadth of experience, they then choose their degree pathway. During subsequent years, students mainly study areas specific to their respective pathway but are also able to choose units which naturally belong to another pathway, thus enabling a student to both specialize and broaden their knowledge. There are currently in excess of 500 students enrolled on the scheme from a wide academic background and age range.

This chapter considers some of the problems, both academic and pastoral, encountered by the course management team and the support needed by students in making their choices. Specifically, a number of decision points are examined in the unitized context. This includes the initial choice of university and degree programme, choice of pathway and options after the first year, whether to undertake an industrial placement year and choices in the final year and beyond. The first two decision points are shown to be especially important. A range of support mechanisms are examined and evaluated and we include results of student feedback.

Between them the authors are course director of the scheme, one of the degree managers and scheme admissions tutor. We are fully involved in both the academic welfare of the scheme and the pastoral care and guidance required by students. Under the direction of the course director there is a strong management team consisting of degree managers, year coordinators and admissions tutor. The management team supports students of various levels of maturity and academic background guiding them through the maze of units enabling them to obtain a degree worthy of their ability.

The department of Information Science at the University of Portsmouth covers a wide range of computing and information systems-based activities. For many years the 'flagship' course was the BSc (Hons) in Computer Science. In 1988 this was considerably broadened into the present Computer Studies degree scheme. Two years ago unitization was imposed upon the scheme.

THE DEGREE SCHEME

The Computer Studies degree scheme (Figure 6.1) starts with a first year which is common to all study pathways. At the start of the second year, students specialize by first choosing from one of the four named honours degree pathways within the scheme and then choosing a selection of options from within the chosen pathway and beyond. The range of choice covers technical computing, business and humanities subjects. The degree scheme is available in four-year sandwich mode with a fall back of three years full-time mode for unplaced students.

The four named degree pathways are: Computer Science (CS), Business Information Systems (BIS), Business Information Technology (BIT) and Information Technology and Society (ITS) which span technical, business and humanities subject areas as illustrated in Figure 6.1.

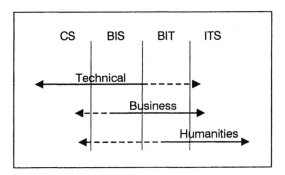

Figure 6.1 *Faculties involved within the scheme*

Scale of the degree scheme

The degree scheme involves three faculties and eight departments with more than 60 lecturing staff. There are 125 units from which students choose 36 over three years; these are taken by approximately 520 students. The scheme also uses some units from other pathways and other degrees use our units.

Unitization

At the University of Portsmouth, most courses are now unitized. The University year consists of two 15-week semesters with an assessment point at the end of each semester. In each semester, students study six units (12 per year).

Management structure

The degree scheme is managed by a course team comprising the course director, four degree managers, four year coordinators and an admissions tutor, as shown in Figure 6.2. Within the management team, there are clearly defined roles for each member. The degree managers are primarily responsible for the academic health of subjects related to their respective degree pathways within the scheme. The year coordinators' roles relate to the organization and administration of their year group. They provide the first port of call for students wishing to discuss both academic and pastoral matters. They are supported in this by a large team of personal tutors, and one member of staff is allocated as personal tutor for each student. In semester one of year one, each tutor meets their tutees weekly in a timetabled 'foundation studies' period which allows time for discussion of group concerns.

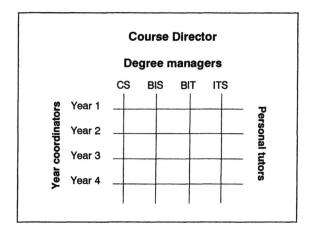

Figure 6.2   *Management structure*

Student choice

Before entry to a university, potential students are faced with a number of difficult decisions. The course team see it as an important part of their support for enabling an effective student learning experience to provide appropriate information and to spend time answering the questions of potential students.

The decisions which potential students face fall under three main headings. Figure 6.3 illustrates this for our degree scheme.

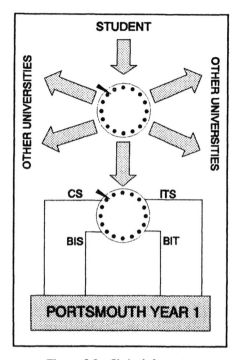

Figure 6.3 *Choice before entry*

Influencing factors here are believed to include distance from home, the location of the university, the facilities provided by the university, availability of living accommodation and recommendation by others.

The admissions tutor for the degree scheme has carried out some research among current students as to why they chose to come to Portsmouth. This was done using a questionnaire at enrolment to avoid answers being influenced by subsequent experience of the university. Results are summarized later and show very clearly that the main reason for choosing a given university is the course itself. Other factors feature far lower in the priority order. This knowledge allows us to design course information packs appropriately.

Which degree course?

It is believed that there are two different types of potential student who have different requirements at this stage of their decision making.

The first type have a very clear idea of the course of study which they are seeking. They frequently require answers to a quite detailed set of questions. At times these questions show that they do not truly appreciate the scope of the discipline which they wish to study, but others do show considerable insight. These people are not satisfied by generalist answers.

The second type usually have a broad idea of the field in which they wish to study but are then looking for courses which fire their enthusiasm. For these people, course information has to take a broader view and should describe what is on offer in a way that sounds bright and interesting.

Without prior knowledge of an inquirer it is a difficult balancing act to interest both groups with the same information.

Since the first year of the scheme is common to all pathways, students are able to reconsider their choice of degree pathway before starting the second year. As this is the case, there is an argument for not presenting applicants with this decision before entry. However, it is felt that by retaining it, the broad nature of the scheme is emphasized to applicants. The general prospectus has a section describing the scheme, but also has information about individual pathways placed in the sections for the appropriate faculties. Internal politics whereby faculties wish to identify 'their students' is also a factor in this decision. Having chosen their degree pathway, students then have to choose from a selection of options from both within the pathway and beyond. These decision points are shown in Figure 6.4.

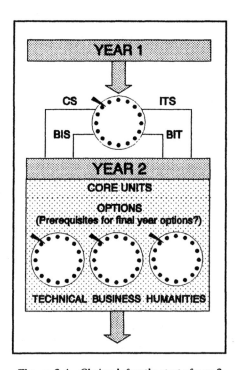

Figure 6.4 *Choice: before the start of year 2*

Experience gained – support and choices before entry

The first point of contact for most potential students is the university general prospectus. This gives the scheme exposure in all appropriate places. Frequent enquiries asking for additional information are received, mainly by telephone. The admissions tutor is available, as far as possible, to deal with these calls. Applicants respond well to being able to speak to a member of the course team. The follow-up is usually to send out a departmental brochure which contains far more information about the scheme than the general prospectus. Subsequently an individual visit is requested in a significant number of cases. These visits are almost entirely dealt with by the admissions tutor. Many of the visitors are potentially mature students and are offering non-standard qualifications and/or experience. Applicants are not normally interviewed; decisions are based on the application form. However, all successful applicants are invited to an open day.

The course team believe that potential students are influenced in their decisions at this stage by a number of factors, namely geographical location, course content, opinions of current students, computing and other facilities, lecturing staff and living accommodation. It is also felt that parents have a significant influence on the final decision made by the potential student. The open day was therefore designed to provide information and contact in these areas for both potential students and their parents.

At the open day they meet current students and staff, including the professor/head of department, who sees this as most important. They then tour the facilities, are taken on a coach trip round the city, given lunch and are talked to about the department, course content and life in Portsmouth. Accompanying parents are also invited to join the open day. In part, these people are seen separately. We believe that parents and potential students want the opportunity to discuss different things.

Following the first year of open days in this format, a feedback survey was undertaken to evaluate the original suppositions.

Results of survey

At enrolment, 158 students joining the degree scheme were asked to rate on a scale of 1 (unimportant) to 4 (very important) six possible reasons for having chosen to come to Portsmouth. By far the most important was course content with 92 per cent rating it at 3 (36 per cent) or 4 (56 per cent). Also high among the priorities was location, followed by the reputation of the university. Relatively low were sports/social facilities and, surprisingly, living accommodation. Recommendation by friends and others was important to only a very few. The departmental brochure was felt by 85 per cent to answer all or most of their questions. However, only about half felt that it had influenced their decision to join us.

They were then asked whether features of the open days influenced their decision. The 'talk about the course' was rated very highly by almost all students, reinforcing their reasons for choosing Portsmouth. Almost as important was 'meeting staff' and the 'welcome'. The 'coach trip' influenced only a few and the biggest surprise in these results was that 'meeting present students' was similarly rated, with only 25 per cent attaching any importance to it.

Inviting parents to join in the open day was a new venture this year. Over 90 per cent of them were thought by their offspring to have been impressed by the event. However, amusingly, no student admitted to having been strongly influenced in their decision by their accompanying parents following the open day visit. (The authors suspect that the students may possibly not be totally truthful here.)

Students who had made an individual visit were asked if this had influenced them. Almost every student making such a visit gave a top rating to 'friendly welcome' and 'questions fully answered'. Almost 90 per cent thought that their visit had greatly influenced their decision.

In summary, 62 per cent of applicants coming to an open day subsequently joined us as students. Seventy of those surveyed had joined following an individual visit. From these results it would appear that an open friendly approach by an admissions tutor who is available as much as possible, together with an awareness of the results above allow the course team of the scheme to be responsive to the needs of potential students making difficult decisions. Meeting government MASN student targets is also aided!

Based on this one cohort of 158 students, it would appear that many of the original suppositions were valid (Wilson, 1994). The real surprise was that 'meeting staff' was seen to be much more important than 'meeting current students'. For this following year, the same format has been retained and further feedback data will be obtained.

Experience gained – support and choices after one year

As students approach the end of their first year, they are faced with what are arguably the most important decisions of their degree: choice of degree pathway and choice of options. The provision of adequate support at this point is relatively expensive in resource terms. However, the course team believe that such support is justified for the following reasons (Wheeler and Birtle, 1993).

> Students who choose effectively are more likely to enjoy their studies, complete their course and obtain a degree worthy of their ability.
>
> Students who fail to choose effectively are more likely to:

- fail at some stage
- drop out before completion
- distract other students
- perform poorly
- require subsequent support which is costly in staff time.

A range of considerations appear to influence student selections. These include:

- performance so far

- content

- personalities (staffing)

- peer pressure (not to be underestimated)

- perception that some subjects are 'easy'

- assessment methods

- effects on final-year choices

- accreditation by professional bodies.

The following support structure is believed to give students the opportunity to 'get it right'. Support has two aspects: what to provide and when. The present system has evolved over several years and is successful judging by student reaction to it.

Information is provided in four ways: in writing; by staff to groups of students; by staff to individuals; and by other students. When to provide this information is perceived by the course team to be equally important.

Students are initially provided with a 'year-two course book' at the start of the Easter holiday. The course book provides them with a picture of the overall structure of the scheme, including the final year. It tells them which subjects are core units and which optional in each degree pathway in the second and final years and indicates diagrammatically which year-two subjects are prerequisite to which final year subjects. The book also contains unit descriptions for all year-two subjects which gives the answers to content and assessment questions. The name of the author of the unit description is shown, but at that stage the lecturer for the unit is not necessarily known. The aim is to give students the opportunity to consider their choices away from intense peer pressure. Students are encouraged to discuss their ideas at home with their families and many do so.

On their return, a group session is provided to outline the choices and answer any general questions which have arisen. Invariably the intricacies of professional accreditation require further explanation. This is subsequently followed by an informal arranged opportunity to discuss the second year with students from each degree pathway. Coffee is provided and staff withdraw. Students find this opportunity most useful.

Two weeks are then allowed to give students a chance to consider. During this period, staff expect to spend time individually with students. Option choice forms are then expected to be returned to allow timetabling to begin. Students may change their minds later, up to two weeks after the start of the Autumn term, but new choices may then only be made within the constraints of the timetable, room sizes and laboratory accommodation. Only a very few do change at this late stage, suggesting that the support provided is working. Those who do change late on tend to be the weaker students who will require continuing individual support.

Industrial placement year

The course team see the industrial placement year as an important and integral part of a student's studies. From the department's viewpoint, students on placement are also students who do not have to be taught, thus effectively improving the SSR position. Staff also visit students on placement which provides useful industrial contact.

The benefits of this year for the student are seen to be:

- maturity
- experience
- money – at the time and possibly during the final year
- employment opportunities after graduation
- greater benefit from the final year
- valuable source of final-year projects.

During the second year students have to make a choice of whether they are intending to undertake an industrial placement year. Figure 6.5 illustrates the decision points at this stage and shows the effect of the different choices.

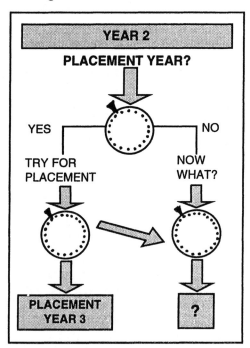

Figure 6.5 *Choice: industrial placement year*

At this point, students require individual advice although a weekly timetabled session is available for each degree pathway for this purpose. These sessions give students the chance to discuss the world of work, job application procedures and interview techniques with the industrial placement officer. They are in competition with students from other universities and need continuing guidance. As employment opportunities arise it is the responsibility of each individual student to put themselves forward for consideration.

Students who do not take part in the placement exercise, or who do so and are unsuccessful, have to decide whether to continue directly to the final year or to take a year out from their studies. Those who do not take part in the exercise invariably decide to go directly to the final year without advice. They are usually mature students who have substantial work experience before joining the scheme. About half of the remaining students tend to take a break in their studies, preferring to complete the course with their peers and again require individual support in this decision, often in the middle of the summer vacation. Some students see lack of success in the placement exercise as a failure on their behalf and take considerable persuasion to view the situation in a positive light.

The final year

Irrespective of whether a student takes the industrial training placement year, they will all follow the same final year course. At this stage they will have to make choices about which options to take, though a substantial number of the option choices available to a student will be dependent on prerequisite units taken during the second year. Figure 6.6 shows the final year choices.

Influences here are:

- prerequisites

- peer pressure

- personalities

- future career direction

- degree classification expectations – some subjects are perceived as 'easy'.

A project topic also has to be selected; this is a major component of the final year.

By this time, most students are self-sufficient in their decision-making, requiring only option information. Project topics are however often discussed. Students who undertake a placement year can consider these matters during that year. Each student is visited twice in their placement which provides an opportunity for discussion. Many placement students also have easy access to staff using e-mail. Placement employers are often very willing to provide project topics for their trainees and frequently then support the student during the project period.

Students who do not undertake a placement miss both the period for decision-making and the exposure to project ideas. It is these students who need individual support in the last weeks before the start of the final year, and frequently during that year.

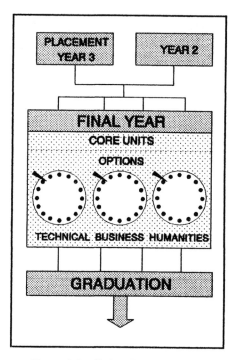

Figure 6.6 *Choice: final year options*

Having successfully completed the degree scheme on one of the four pathways and graduated, students will once again have to choose between continuing education and a career. This is shown in Figure 6.7.

Many sources of advice are available to students approaching graduation and afterwards, including the university careers service and the department. At this stage of their careers, students are expected to be self-motivated and seek advice when they deem it necessary. Within the department, course managers and students' personal tutors have an important role here. Last year 95 per cent of our graduates found employment or progressed to further study.

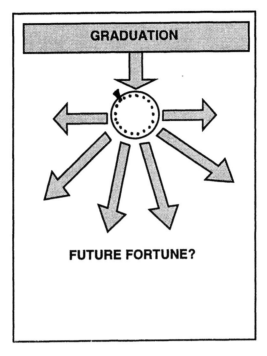

Figure 6.7 *Choice after graduation*

CONCLUSION

Unitization has increased flexibility of study for students but has also increased the scope for choosing unwisely. The level of formal and informal support required by students under unitization has risen significantly in quality and frequency as compared with the previous non-unitized course structure.

In the degree scheme examined, support for decisions made before, during and after year one are shown to be particularly crucial. The support mechanisms developed by the course team, involving a combination of paper- and people-based information, have enabled most students to make appropriate choices throughout their programme of study. In developing these mechanisms there have been two main targets: enabling students to choose effectively and optimizing the use of staff time and other resources. The current systems have been shown to be working well. The key to this success is the clearly structured management team and the way in which its members communicate with the students throughout their time in Portsmouth and afterwards. No student need ever feel that they are alone and lost in this maze of choice.

REFERENCES

Wilson, S T (1994) *Feedback from students at enrolment*, internal publication, University of Portsmouth, Department of Information Science.

Wheeler, S and Birtle, J (1993) *A Handbook for Personal Tutors*, Open University Press, Buckingham.

Chapter 7

Use of the Study Support Service

Keith Guest

INTRODUCTION

This chapter explains the philosophy and operation of a study support service as centrally provided within the University of Luton. The service includes 'in-course' provision, discrete modules and a drop-in workshop which is available to all students. An analysis of student drop-in and perception of this provision is provided as a basis for evaluation and discussion.

The rationale behind providing a drop-in service at the University has been, from the first, student-led. This initiative started life as a project within the Centre for Educational Development (CED) to provide back-up, in terms of systems, to the instigation of general skills support across the institution. As part of the programme of support mechanisms, we were concerned to investigate the feasibility and practicality of running such a system and to provide our colleagues with a working model which would be directly transferable to their field/specialism. Thus, the first two years were concerned with numbers attending, preference for times of access and so on, and this was staffed fully by CED lecturers interested in researching this type of provision. Our research interest continues, specifically into how to better integrate the acquisition of study skills into a modular scheme.

> UK government projections anticipate over a million full-time equivalent students in Higher Education in Great Britain by 2000 ('Higher Education A New Framework'). For these numbers to be achieved, Higher Education institutions increasingly will have to cater for the needs of adults, part-time students and younger men and women whose prior experience and aspirations might, in the past, have excluded them from Higher Education – either because they were not formally qualified for entry or because they may not have perceived Higher Education as relevant to them (PCFC, 1992).

This will have a familiar ring to all who have been involved in the provision of support systems in institutions of further and higher education, as we get to grips with rethinking and reforming attitudes towards learning and learners, (and, incidentally, their attitudes towards us). Some changes in the perception these 'new' students have of the role of lecturers has led many practitioners in HE to question the traditional approach to their task. In particular, the growth in non-standard entries has raised important questions about how we assess ability (or potential) in HE and how we support this new (and wider) range of learning styles.

This growth in the range of students, in terms of ethnic mix, sex, age and qualifications entering HE in the past few years has been striking, perhaps typified in the general growth in the new universities such as Luton. The situation can be summed up by a general bemusement, both on the part of the students finding themselves suddenly in an environment they had not previously considered, and on the part of academic staff finding themselves coping with people they might once have considered non-academic.

The philosophy underlying the provision of study skills at the University of Luton remains as it always was: that students attending this institution reflect the more general trend in education evident over a number of years towards competence-based and vocational courses which may, in certain cases, result in some of the building blocks for higher study being underdeveloped. The trend most obvious in non-standard entries is mirrored in post-A level students to a greater or lesser degree according to individual experience. The students themselves recognise their shortcomings and, while some are both highly motivated and able, others seek clearer direction from the institution.

The following analyses are taken from a survey of students at induction in 1994. The team was concerned to elicit the students' opinion of their own abilities/shortcomings as a basis for comparison with staff perceptions and as a foundation for institutional responses. A maximum of 257 freshers completed our survey which asked them to express their opinion as to their readiness for HE in terms of the skills they would be called upon to use during their time as undergraduates.

What is clear from the students' own assessments is that there are particularly noticeable weaknesses in some of the areas we traditionally hold as essential in HE: less than 40 per cent are confident in applying problem-solving techniques, less than 20 per cent are confident in presentations, note-taking and time management. The classic areas of written assignments produced a not-unexpected response of less than 50 per cent confidence, whether it be essays, reports, or any other form of written assessment. Clearly, there are some real issues in written communications which need to be addressed. (The drop-in service affects the tip of the iceberg but, with so general a problem, we cannot take on the responsibility across the board.) The age range of our students may play some part in this uneasiness with traditional academic approaches, although most had been involved with academic work recently (remembering that this includes those who have progressed from the foundation year 0). Of the more innovative forms of assessment (such as reflective journals), the students knew little (8 per cent).

Not surprisingly, perhaps, very few students thought that all assignments should be word-processed, but this contrasts markedly with the general trend amongst lecturers. Some 55 per cent of new students had used computers but less than 18 per cent were familiar with Apple Macintosh. The highest use of computers was, unsurprisingly, for games. In the students' rating of their own level of skills, a total of 73 per cent claimed only basic skills or absolute beginner (28 per cent). A very small minority (20 per cent) thought themselves fairly proficient, while less than 3 per cent claimed to be very proficient. In all cases, word-processing or spreadsheet, more than half the students who responded to our survey said they required workshop assistance.

The experience at Luton could easily reflect the national experience and a glance at the local impact of Access provision gives an idea of the picture beginning to emerge. Access, in this context, refers to courses provided for adults (21+) who have previously been excluded from studying at HE level because they had not achieved the 'standard' entry requirements for those courses. Typically, this will include students from the following categories: those who left school at 15 or 16 without taking any exams; those who have been at home raising a family; part-time workers or unemployed persons seeking to improve their qualifications (and hence their job prospects); and single parents whose children have now moved into full-time education. In 1993, within the Bedfordshire Access Consortium, there were some 660 students following 21 Access routes. At that time, many of these courses were redesignated as Level 'O' of HE courses at the University of Luton, this being the foundation year of a four-year programme of study. Access provision has thus gained significant numbers, is part of the mainstream, and emphasizes the ever-closer links between the universities and the workplace. An illustration of the projected growth in this area is shown in Figure 7.1 (Bedfordshire Access Consortium, 1993).

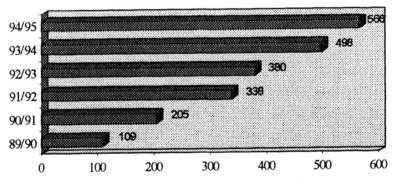

Figure 7.1 *Planned growth of Access 1989/95*

Whether or not we wish to question the reliability of A levels as predictors of performance in HE, or academic success in general (cf. The Robins Report,

1963), for this fast-increasing number of students, or A levels as 'count norms' is not relevant. Nevertheless, questions must be asked covering some of the fundamental aims and objectives in HE and has been instrumental in the development of new syllabi and strategies for delivery. This has included strategies to promote the acquisition of transferable generic skills which will be relevant to all courses and includes also higher level imaginative and evaluative skills as well as those carrying a 'remedial' tag, from using the library to essay writing.

Those of us involved in educational development have often carried the responsibility of developing these strategies on behalf of our colleagues across the institution and several approaches have been tried. Here at Luton, the Access students followed a core syllabus, targeting 'study skills', covering the basic competences while promoting enquiry and research. They use, for example, problem-solving techniques to develop student-centred approaches to learning, that is the lecturer presents a model which is then practised, leading to a discussion (and often a new/modified model) (Frederick, 1989). This approach echoes the modular scheme format and there is currently some debate as to the viability of adopting a foundation module or even semester at level 1. Another strategy has been the setting up of drop-in workshops available to all students on demand. During 1993/94, the service was staffed from noon to 5pm every day with one late night, till 7pm, on Thursdays and covered maths/numeracy and basic IT as well as communication skills.

The idea was to always have one member of staff representing each discipline covered by the drop-in service on hand during opening times. Thus, we aimed to have IT cover, maths and communications cover operating at the same time. In order to provide students with the maximum choice in drop-in, it is necessary to keep long hours of opening, even though this can ultimately lead to some periods of under-use. However, the location of the service in the same building as the team's personal offices has allowed some doubling up under an 'on-call' system. This 'best of both worlds' approach, timetabled drop-in coupled with the 'on-call' system, has proved effective in allowing students choice in attendance times with a comparatively small human resource base. This might well provide a model for future development, expansion onto other campuses, subject or field specific provision, and so on.

In workshops, students discussed their work and the problems they met. (Those who thought we were going to do the work for them were sadly disappointed.) We were particularly interested in the development of higher-order thinking skills through directed practice in reading, listening and analysing as part of a group or one-to-one, with the teacher being an integral part of the process, leading to interactive discussion and evaluation.

Emphasis was firmly put on referral to the original source; each lecturer has a preferred style which must be built on top of generic writing skills. So, for example, if a student came in with an assignment, we would begin by referring to the title or cover sheet which would often contain quite detailed criteria for completion of the assignment: number of words, layout and style, even some 'leading' questions to be addressed. Of course, not all students would bring their work at this early stage; some would bring first or even second drafts of their work for a quick second opinion before handing it in.

In these cases the approach was the same (even though occasionally frustrating for the student): refer to first base – who is it for? What special instructions have they given? Two further questions were then used: where did you get your information? How did you sort out that information into a usable plan? These generally led to open discussion on areas the individual student recognized as a problem and which could then be shown to have had an affect on the production of the assignment. For example, a student who did not use the library effectively would tend not to back up their work with referenced materials or might simply 'stick in' a quote and hope that would do the trick. The involvement of the lecturer as a sounding board acted as a prompt to the students identifying their own problems so that these could then be addressed effectively.

> Hearing the lecturer 'think out aloud' about a problem or issue is a vital way of helping students to understand the discipline. In first year classes, basic subject-specific study skills techniques can also be taught in this way (Entwistle *et al.*, 1992).

Examples of probing questions commonly used demonstrate the critical thinking processes by which we hoped to encourage their group to evaluate 'knowledge' and generate their own set of answers and ideas.

Probes are used to ask for clarification, that is when a student's answer is too vague or unclear, they may seek meaning or clarification. Questions the students might be asked are, what does the author mean by this statement? Has the author given enough information for us to draw this conclusion?

Probes on critical awareness are used to draw the student out to demonstrate understanding of a concept or reflect on an answer. Similarly, critical thinking skills in HE require the student to question logic, query assumptions, examine analogies and look into the validity of evidence. The support lecturer might make use of questions such as: What are you assuming? Why would that be so? How can that be? How would you do that? Are you sure? Give me an example. What do we need to know in order to solve the problem?

To take one example of these, the support lecturer would first recognize an assumption and question its validity him/herself and then ask the individual/ group if it was safe. This would then lead to other questions, stemming from the group discussion, requiring the lecturer each time to keep an alert mind to stay one step ahead of the group. (Remember, the students' problems would be subject-specific and we do not pretend to be expert in all fields but seek to *apply* transferable generic skills.) A practised lecturer would learn to see a problem coming from some distance ahead, although they would not necessarily steer the group away from it; rather they would allow the mistake, under control, as a learning mechanism. Students would learn to avoid similar mistakes in their future work.

Other probes recommended include refocusing, seeing concepts from another perspective. These encourage the students to question the relevance of evidence within a context and its transferability (How is that related to...?) and tests their understanding of argument (Can you summarize the discussion up to this point?)

Prompting helps the students to recognize conflicting argument within the passage or inconsistent reasoning and leads on to further argumentation (Be more specific. In what way? If that is true, then what if? How would you say that in a different way?) Again, the lecturer must develop the ability to 'see' which way the argument is heading, follow a sometimes slender thread, and recognize potholes in the paths followed. (Examples of probes are adapted from Majer, 1992).

These techniques, which seek to combine specific skills attainment with a problem-solving, student-centred approach, may be said to promote and develop thinking skills. Thus, even basic (or even remedial) work will have real academic value.

On entry to the drop-in workshop, students were asked to fill in details of their name, course and the type of support they required. We also recorded the amount of time they spent using the service at any one time. An analysis of the pattern of use is given in Figure 7.2. Across the institution, there was a peak load problem of assignments due in the weeks just before Christmas. The total numbers of students coming for drop-in help fell significantly after the Christmas break and again after the inter-semester break. The Easter holiday was another example of an interruption to studying, with noticeably less activity after than before. However, there was a corresponding increase in demand for taught sessions to whole classes in, for example, revision and exam techniques.

Weekly Study Support Totals 1993–1994

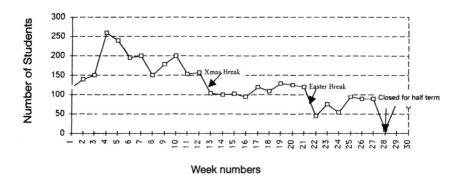

Figure 7.2 *Student numbers arriving for drop-in help on a weekly basis*

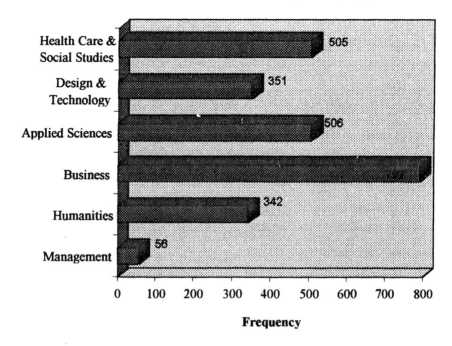

Figure 7.3 *Who are the students?*

The main demand for study support came from the Faculty of Business (see Figure 7.3) with other faculties making fairly equal use of the assistance, with the exception of Management. (The Faculty of Management is situated off campus, some distance from the town centre and has a high percentage of part-time/evening study programmes.)

The level at which the students were studying also varied considerably (see Figure 7.4). Postgraduate students were there mostly for help with research methodology in statistical analysis, or to use the SPSS package within the IT resource; perhaps surprisingly, there was demand for 'basic' writing skills from postgraduate students, although this was requested as a taught course to whole groups rather than as drop-in support. (Perhaps there was some remedial 'tag' perceived in the one-to-one aspect.) Postgraduates may represent a new and growing body of students who need support; for example, we came across science postgraduates who had successfully avoided having to develop any sustained writing skills in their undergraduate courses. Other students working independently, such as students on open learning modules, are an obvious market for the services of study support. Level 0 students made up only one-half of students supported, down from three-quarters last year. This trend appears to be continuing in 1994/95: there has been an increase in uptake from level 2 students, although it should be noted that Humanities have now included workshops as part of the mainstream programme for level 0 courses. (Level 0 includes the full-time Access students as well as foundation courses.) Other HE users are mainly Project 2000 (nursing) students; in the FE sector the main users are design and technology students.

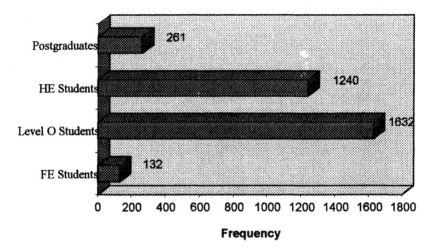

Figure 7.4   *Level of course*

We recorded a total of 3,927 student visits to drop-in workshops during the 1993/94 academic year (an increase of over 1,200 over the year before). It is interesting to note the numbers attending from Humanities, despite a long walk from Castle Street, not by any means all at level 0 and mostly requesting essay-writing support. The 'in-house' workshops encourage participation at all levels. Low numbers from Management, while explainable by the high number of part-time/evening students, remains to be resolved, although much greater in-course skills provision has been considered in curriculum design for these courses.

In deciding the role of the tutor, it is important to identify the competences and skills which are necessary for success in HE, prior to deciding upon a course of action to teach/enhance these skills. In addition, we need to consider other educational factors in deciding what exactly we wish to develop and why. What do we require of HE and what competences should students bring to it as prerequisites and what competences, as educators, should we provide?

Higher Education is about more than even knowledge and skills, let alone skills in their own. It is about educating the whole person, it is about encouraging 'personal growth' and even about facilitating the development of 'wisdom'. There are desired learning outcomes that are not exhausted by listing a set of knowledge, skills and competences with which one purports to equip the student (Wengraf, 1993).

Wengraf echoes the feelings of many educators in concentrating on the 'value-added' aspects of HE and expressing some of the associated problems, that is, that these 'maxi-skills' may be not only difficult to define satisfactorily, but also impossible to guarantee by training – relying more on their facilitation through training, as well as difficult to discriminate between in terms of levels of achievement. These problems apart, Wengraf argues strongly in favour of educators identifying and facilitating the simple skills which go to make up these complex competences and being aware that they are 'more than just the sum of the addition of any number of simple skills (or even the product of the integration)' (ibid.). Hence any programme of study should aim to build on a wide variety of skills and competences which, following the theory of 'critical thinking by association', would best prepare the student for study at a higher level. Incidentally, the question of whether these skills are only preparation for study or have implications for the way in which the student lives his or her life is of importance here. If students on our courses become better thinkers, does this make them better students or better people? Again, this refers to values in HE and in a wider sphere.

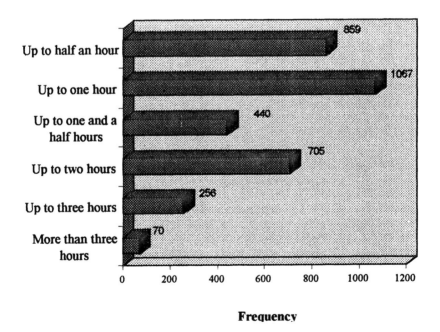

Frequency

Figure 7.5 *The length of time students study*

The centre was open for 25 hours a week (each afternoon) and involved four lecturers (two FTE). A weighted average shows the typical student spent 1 hour 20 minutes in the drop-in centre for each visit (see Figure 7.5). The 3,927 student visits therefore represent over 5,000 hours of delivery. Is this in itself a measure of success? Anecdotal evidence suggests that the students like the service and we are engaging in further research (including a comparison of 'before and after' performances) to try to establish whether and in what way they may benefit from it. Staff too seem to appreciate the referral possibilities. During the 1994/95 academic year, our focus is much more on the effectiveness of a variety of alternative models for skills delivery, in terms of cost to the institution and how well they meet the requirements of staff and students alike. Certainly, in our opinion, we have shown the value of a 'safety-net' approach by simply having somewhere the students can go and talk to someone; we hope it's an idea that will catch on.

The past three years have stressed the importance of recognizing the existence of a generic study problem, first amongst the staff and second amongst the student body. It was clear from an early stage that the students were usually aware of their own shortcomings, but did not want the admission of these to in any way influence their chances of acceptance into HE. Hence, the problems were largely underplayed, if not ignored, and there was reluctance to go for help to those who were actively involved in their general assessment. This has been one of the strengths of the open drop-in safety net and adds to, rather than detracts from, the specific workshops which are part of in-course provision.

REFERENCES

Bedfordshire Access Consortium (1993) *Periodic Review*, Volume 1, pp.7, 8.

Entwistle *et al.* (1992) *Guidelines for Promoting Effective Learning in Higher Education*, University of Edinburgh, Centre for Research on Learning and Instruction, pp.25–30, 35–9.

Frederick, P J (1989) 'Involving students more actively in the classroom', *New Directions for Teaching and Learning*, 37, Jossey-Bass, San Francisco.

Majer, K (1992) *Retention: Keeping Your Students in the 80's*, in UMKC SI leader training manual, p.28.

PCFC (1992) *Widening Participation in Higher Education*, Report of a Study of Polytechnics and Colleges of Higher Education in England, PCFC, Bristol.

Robins (1963) *Higher Education*, Report of the Committee chaired by Lord Robins, HMSO, London.

Wengraf, T (1993) 'Policy or skills development', *Learning Action Bulletin*, Spring, pp.11–6.

SECTION TWO:
Strategies and Support for Undergraduate and Postgraduate Teaching and Learning

Chapter 8

Can You Teach an Old Dog New Tricks? Student Induction on an HND Extension Degree

Clare Brindley and Peter Cuthbert

INTRODUCTION TO THE PROBLEM

In common with many other of the new universities, Manchester Metropolitan (MMU) offers students the chance to build upon their Higher National Diploma (HND) qualification and read for a degree. Within the Department of Business and Management Studies at Crewe and Alsager Faculty, there are three linked degrees offering two-year extension programmes. The degrees have the standard MMU Credit Accumulation and Transfer (CATs) structure and are made up of six modules per year. Of these modules, three are common in each year, with the remainder being specific to the degree route. The common modules are taught as mass lectures with smaller tutorial follow-up groups. The routes are BA (Hons) Business, Sport and Recreation, BA (Hons) Business, Leisure and Recreation and the BA (Hons) Business Administration, colloquially known as BABSR, BABLR and BABA. These three degrees recruit approximately 100 students from an internal market of around 300 HND students, plus students from other institutions.

The 'three degrees' course team perceived that there was a very different culture in degree work compared to diploma work and so a problem of change would be faced by the ex-HND students. This view was supported by the very first cohort of Business, Sport and Recreation degree students who reported the need for some form of induction programme. This degree recruited its first cohort in 1992/93 while the other two degrees recruited their first cohorts in 1993/94.

The underlying rationale for the induction programme was to encourage students to adopt a more meaning-oriented approach to studying. Staff involved in the programme wished to make the issue of differences in approach between HND studies and degree studies explicit and hence influence students' habits.

DIFFERENCES BETWEEN DEGREE AND HND

As a starting point for planning the induction programme, the course team informally sought the views of colleagues who taught both on diploma and degree routes. Most colleagues reported that the HND is more vocationally oriented than the degree route. However, when pressed, colleagues were unable to point to specific and quantifiable differences between the routes. In an attempt to classify the differences, the structure for analysis of curriculum styles and strategies proposed by Heathcote *et al.* (1988) was used. The structure proposes four headings:

● Curriculum intentions

● Organization of the curriculum content

● Instructional procedures

● Assessment and grading.

Curriculum intentions

Under this heading it was found that there was little difference between the routes. It is likely that the current pressure to adopt a standard university style for course definitions will lead to even smaller differences in the future.

Organization of the curriculum content

In the early days of the Business Education Council (BEC) and Technical Education Council (TEC) awards there was considerable pressure to move away from traditional 'subjects' and integrate curriculum content under a series of key themes. Typical of the pressure was the development of the composite topic 'Business Environment'. The curricula for the degrees and the HND showed no significant differences in this area. The degrees contained a number of composite modules and similarly the HND contains a number of traditional subject modules.

Instructional procedures

Heathcote *et al.* (op.cit.) divide this heading into four categories, of which three are appropriate to this discussion:

– *The Exposition-Discovery Learning Dimension.* Colleagues reported very little difference in the way that the acquisition of curriculum material was achieved on both the degrees and the HND. A common complaint was that pressure of numbers was forcing delivery into the mass lecture mode against the tutors' wishes.

– *The Experiential-Non-experiential Dimension.* It was at this point that the first significant difference emerged. Again tutors provided students with both experiential and non-experiential learning situations. On both routes, the preference of tutors appears to be for experiential learning but there appears to be a difference in emphasis. There is an expectation for degree students that they will bring to any problem a broad background of theoretical knowledge derived from reading round the topic. In the case of HND students, it is usual to expect students to adopt a pragmatic approach to problem-solving in line with the Business and Technical Education Council (BTEC) Common Skills philosophy. The theoretical structures used are normally based upon those identified by the tutors in class and specified reading.

– *Teacher Control-Student Control of the Learning Outcome.* A further difference is that the degrees place great emphasis on assessments being open-ended so that every student can arrive at their own unique solution. This also occurs on the HND, but there are more occasions when the learning outcome is highly teacher-specified.

Assessment and grading

Under this heading, some more differences emerged. The HND uses both course work and examinations while the degrees are continuously assessed except for the language modules. However, this difference is peculiar to the three degrees within the department. Most other degrees in the faculty include examinations for grading purposes.

The assessment of the curriculum differences, while identifying some possible problem areas, was rather less clear cut than had been expected. The much quoted 'vocational orientation' of HND was not identifiable using the chosen tool.

The only other major difference appeared to be in the initial entry qualifications for the HND compared to three-year degree routes elsewhere in the faculty.

The HND requires one A level or equivalent while two A levels or equivalent is needed for a three-year degree. However, even this distinction was complicated by the small number of students entering HND with two A levels or good Ordinary National Diploma (OND) grades. Anecdotal evidence from colleagues also suggested that there is little difference between the 'average' HND student and the 'average' degree student. A large part of any difference seems to depend upon the individual student's motivation and interest in the subject.

The issue of motivation and effort has also been mentioned by the HND students themselves. They often confess to having lacked commitment and effort in their studying at school, and blamed this on their 'poor' A level results. Since the induction programme was for ex-HND students entering an extension degree route, it was felt that this issue of students' commitment and approaches to study might be worth considering.

The extensive literature on the topic (eg, Entwistle and Ramsden, 1983; Richardson, 1990; Gibbs, 1992) suggests that students are likely to adopt one of two, or possibly three, approaches to studying. The meaning approach, in which the student has the intention to understand and internalize the material, is considered to be the most appropriate and desirable for undergraduates (Gow and Kember, 1990). The reproducing approach, where the student has the intention to get by with as little understanding as possible, is considered to be undesirable. A third possibility, the strategic approach, is postulated by Entwistle (op. cit.), but disputed by Richardson (op. cit.). Whether the adoption of a meaning approach is beneficial to the student's grading performance is still a matter of debate and will probably depend upon the form of assessment used. Ely (1992) found that a meaning approach was beneficial, while Beckwith (1991) took the opposite view.

As part of a different investigation, the Richardson version of Entwistle's Approaches to Study Inventory (ASI) had been completed by a number of both first- and second-year HND students in October 1992. It was also completed by the new intake to the extension degrees in October 1994. As was expected the results for the two groups were similar for all the constructs and the differences were not statistically significant at the 0.05 level. The general picture was of fairly low scores on the meaning approach and high scores on the reproducing approach. Hidden within these figures were a number of individuals with high meaning scores, but who also had relatively high reproducing scores.

On the basis of these two sets of ASI scores, and the Business, Sport and Recreation degree's end of year evaluation, the 'three degrees' team identified the following as the requirements of the induction programme for ex-HND students:

- organizational issues – this includes the way the course operates, assessment, course regulations, the personal tutor system, personal issues like time management and the personal portfolio;

- study skills – the need to adopt more effective study habits than were exhibited on HND;

- course philosophy – the courses were designed round the image of the 'reflective practitioner' or 'capability' concept where the student takes responsibility for their own learning. This is somewhat different to the paternalism of the HND.

THE FIRST INDUCTION PROGRAMME

Approach

The first induction programme was designed and prepared by a small group comprising the course leaders, the HND common skills coordinator, and two other staff. The student representatives from the previous year's Sports degree were consulted before the group had a brainstorming session to derive the initial programme. The draft was then circulated to the whole team for comments and volunteers to staff the programme were requested. Following this, the final programme was decided upon. It was not considered necessary to organize a formal induction for the level three Sports group.

Structure

The faculty requires all the students to register, and to be introduced to student and computer services and the libraries before they are released to course-specific inductions. The necessity to comply with these requirements and the number of issues that needed to be included in our specific induction programme could not be accommodated in a single week. In addition, the research into student learning has shown (Entwistle and Ramsden op.cit.) that too pressurized an environment will lead students to fall back into a surface approach to learning. A two-week induction programme was therefore scheduled. This allowed a reasonable amount of self-managed time to be included.

Content

As mentioned earlier, the programme was intended to try to encourage students to adopt a more meaning approach to studying as well as making explicit the course philosophy. A major element in this philosophy is to encourage students to take an active role in the process of assessment. With this in mind, a session on the process of assessment and grading and an exercise in peer assessment was scheduled.

Table 8.1   *Induction Programme 1 – Week One*

Day	Slot 1	Slot 2	Slot 3	Slot 4
Monday	Faculty-organised registration session.	Faculty-organized ID photo session.		
Tuesday	Timetables. Issue of student handbooks and induction programme.		Meet course leader. Intro to course philosophy. Icebreaker exercises.	
Wednesday	Selection of option routes and electives. Complete Belbin Team Roles Quest.	Discussion of results. Tutor input on group dynamics.	Intro to student services. Intro to computer services.	
Thursday	Tutor input on use of library for research. Referencing and sources.	Mixed cohort work groups formed. Choose report topic out of hat.	Small group library intro tours.	Groups start research for reports.
Friday	Tutor input on note taking and precis skills.			

Table 8.2   *Induction Programme 1 – Week Two*

Day	Slot 1	Slot 2	Slot 3	Slot 4
Monday			Tutor input on analysis of information and writing.	
Tuesday	Groups prepare and word process 1,500-word reports.	Groups prepare and word process 1,500-word reports.	Groups prepare and word process 1,500-word reports.	Groups prepare and word process 1,500-word reports.

Day	Slot 1	Slot 2	Slot 3	Slot 4
Wednesday	Lecture on assessment and grading including peer assessment.	Presentation by professional body. (ILAM)	Reports handed in. Procedure for peer assessment explained.	Groups assess work of two other groups using issued assessment sheets.
Thursday	Groups assess work of two other groups using issued assessment sheets.		Feedback of reports and marks. Plenary session on peer assessment.	
Friday	End of course evaluation session using questionnaire.	Free buffet lunch.		

Evaluation

Following the induction programme, the team undertook an evaluation exercise using student questionnaires; the results can be seen in Appendix 1. Overall the team were disappointed that the students were so critical of the programme. Reflecting on this, the team came up with the following observations:

- The induction programme lacked pace and there was too much free time.

- Students perceived that they were 'old hands' and therefore had little to learn about 'studenting' skills. Many students showed a lack of commitment to the induction programme.

- A number of the staff perceived the programme as the course leaders' 'problem' and hence gave it a low priority. Some even did not turn up for their timetabled sessions.

- There was dissatisfaction with the teaching accommodation.

- The use of peer assessment was a failure.

- The level three students felt that they needed an induction programme too.

- The careers service felt that students were not utilizing opportunities for summer placements or job search assistance.

THE SECOND INDUCTION

Approach

Taking on board these observations the course leaders felt that the approach to the following year's induction needed to be radically different. Abandoning the induction programme altogether was not a viable option, but the evaluation highlighted serious deficiencies that needed to be rectified. Consequently the approach to the second induction programme was rather different.

First the course leaders arranged an informal meeting with the student representatives for the three courses away from the university campus. The aim of this meeting was wider than induction. It was felt important to explore the perceptions of the course and those issues that were important from the perspectives of both students and staff. Issues that were discussed included the role and responsibilities of student representatives, assessment workload, staff workload and expectations of students, facilities and the opportunities for change, enhancements and induction.

Many things emerged from this meeting that have been beneficial to the smooth running of the courses. A procedure for student representatives, a revised assessment schedule, and a greater understanding of each other's problems were significant achievements. It also emerged that the student representatives would be more than willing to participate in planning the next level two induction course.

A new approach and the course leaders' wish to reduce the criticisms meant that a new induction planning team was required. It was decided that a wider-ranging membership would be more appropriate. Consequently the student representatives were invited to the planning meeting for the 1994/95 induction courses along with faculty careers officer, library, other interested course team members, the course leaders, and linked pattern leaders (other courses share some 'three degrees' modules).

At the first meeting of the planning group held in the summer term, the contents of the previous induction course were discussed and participants were asked to identify any significant omissions.

Content

As before, the underlying rationale for the level two programme was to encourage students to adopt a more meaning-oriented approach to studying. For level three, the underlying rationale was to prepare students for the greater degree of self-managed learning required in the honours year. A second issue was to provoke students into reflection about the opportunities open to them upon graduation.

The groups' discussion was extensive and, keeping in mind the underlying rationales for the induction programme, each group member contributed to drawing up a list of topics. Armed with this list, details of the faculty induction timetable, and the previous evaluation data, the course leaders drew up a draft induction timetable. The issue of differences in approach between HND study and degree study was not made as explicit, but tasks were arranged to help students come to this conclusion. This timetable was circulated to the planning group for comments and provisional staffing arrangements were made.

Table 8.3 *Induction Programme Two – Level Two*

Day	Slot 1	Slot 2	Slot 3	Slot 4
Monday		Faculty-organised ID photo session.	Meet course leader. Timetables. Option presentations.	Ice breaker: treasure hunt followed by afternoon tea.
Tuesday	Small group library intro tours.	Small group library intro tours.	Faculty-organized registration session.	Intro to student services. Intro to computer services.
Wednesday	Lecture: references and sources.	Practical session on CD-ROM with help from Level 3 students.	Note taking and essay writing session.	Distribution of essay titles, and generic essay feedback sheet.
Thursday	Self-managed time (also need to visit personal tutor).	Self-managed time (also need to visit personal tutor).	Self-managed time (also need to visit personal tutor).	Hand in essays at 4pm prompt.
Friday	Careers service talk on sponsorship and placements.	Lecture on assessment and grading. Return of marked essays.		

Structure

The induction programme was designed to take place over one week with the majority of the first two days given over to faculty induction procedures. In parallel with the level two induction, a separate level three programme was introduced for the first time. As in the previous year, the three degree cohorts were combined, except for their first meetings with their respective course leaders. Due to the rather full timetable, students had very little free time. For the level three students, induction included more self-managed time.

Evaluation

After the induction programmes student questionnaires were issued as part of the evaluation exercise; the results can be seen in Appendices 2 and 3. Again there was plenty of criticism, but the original issues at level two were less in evidence:

● The lack of pace, too much free time and 'old hands' problem seem to have been resolved. This is probably due to the shorter programme, heavier individual task-loading and by not being explicit about the content of timetable sessions in advance. Peer assessment was eliminated.

● The course leaders took on induction as their 'problem' and were responsible for operating most of the sessions.

● The dissatisfaction with the teaching accommodation was not resolved.

The new criticisms at level two revolved around three main areas:

● Students that were new to the faculty felt that they were 'lost' and that insufficient attention had been paid to their needs.

● There was a feeling that more of the induction programme could be run on a degree cohort basis rather than grouped as 'three degrees'.

● More time should be allowed for completing the paper writing task and providing feedback.

Criticisms at level three were somewhat reminiscent of those at level two in the previous year:

● The timetable was perceived as not being well organized.

● Classroom accommodation was considered to be unsatisfactory.

● It was questioned whether it was really necessary to have an induction for level three students.

DISCUSSION

The original rationale for the induction programme was that the approach to study required of undergraduates is different to that required of HND students. This assumption is based upon the views of colleagues, plus a pilot study in 1990/91 that compared the approaches to studying of a sample of BEd students and a sample of HND students. In this case the groups were found to be different in their aggregate meaning scores and aggregate reproducing scores on the ASI, significant at the 0.05 level.

A further study with a bigger sample based solely on 'three degrees' students was carried out during the induction week. It was assumed that the newly recruited students would still have an HND approach to studying. Similarly it was assumed that the students who had just started level three should have adopted an undergraduate approach to studying. The results from this study, while not bearing out the exact results of the pilot study, show results in the expected direction. The differences were found to be in the aggregate meaning scores, which may suggest that the level three students have begun to develop an 'improved' approach. However, the course evaluation for these students after their level two year showed that they found a serious problem with workload. Entwistle and Ramsden (1983) argue that excessive workloads can lead students to adopt a reproducing approach, which is probably the case for our students.

The results from the ASI data support our view that an induction programme can help students to convert from their HND approach to the undergraduate approach. However, it is not possible to claim that the induction programme is, on its own, responsible for this conversion. The data for the level two students was collected just after the induction course and shows them to be still operating in 'HND mode'.

The evaluation questionnaire results for the level two induction show a change of focus from the previous year. Students seem to think that the content of the programme was relevant to their needs, with the paper writing exercise being an exemplar. However, we still need to refine the programme in the light of our admissions policy that aims to recruit more students from outside the faculty. The small numbers of externally sourced students have reported that they suffered from lack of specific attention to their different needs.

The issue of group identity was discussed by the course leaders for the first induction programme, but the cohort sweatshirt and student society initiatives were not taken up by the students. However, the level two course evaluation and the evaluation of the second level two induction seems to suggest that a few students desire a stronger cohort identity. This desire is manifested by calls for separate teaching and separate induction programmes.

At level three we still have some way to go before the programme is satisfactory. Many students questioned the relevance of the final year induction, feeling that the time would have been better spent on modular lectures. This cohort appears to be convinced that they have the necessary skills to cope with their honours year, despite the worries expressed by some of the course team that this is not so. It could be that these students have adopted the approach of taking responsibility for their own learning that has been stressed on the course. Alternatively anecdotal evidence suggests that self-managed time was not effectively utilized by the students.

The careers sessions and the guest lectures were appreciated by some students, but it is not clear whether these were the same students that felt level three induction was useful. The choice of speakers was rather undermined by staff illness and timetable changes which may have contributed to the rather low satisfaction with this element.

SOME RECOMMENDATIONS

It is somewhat pretentious to attempt to generalize too widely from such a small investigation. However, we feel that others may wish to consider our views if only to compare them with their own experience. Using the framework suggested in the circular to presenters at the 1994 Improving Student Learning Symposium we would suggest the following.

Motivational context

The contents of the induction course need to be perceived by the students as being useful for the main course. There is a risk with 'worthy' items like library use and writing that the 'been there, done that' syndrome will undermine the initial enthusiasm of being on a new course. We should use existing students to sell the topics, or set tasks that clearly demonstrate to the students their lack of existing competence. Above all we should try to make it interesting! The unsolved problem is to get teaching teams to realize that induction is just as much part of the course as their subject lectures.

Learner activity

While passive lectures are inevitable in both induction and the main course, it is important to build in as much activity to the programme as possible. The transition from the more activity-based HND to more cerebral degree work is difficult, so we should not expect students to do it too soon. Providing plenty to do will not cause a problem. Nevertheless, there will be complaints that Students Union freshers' events, sport and social events mean there is not enough time. This will help to reinforce the need for good time management.

Interaction

Providing opportunities for student interaction is important for two reasons. First, the new students need to be integrated with the 'old hands' from the in-house HND and second, some form of cohort identity needs to be fostered. Ex-HND students are usually good at group work but our experience is that they are reluctant to move out of friendship groups. Rotating group activities may help to address this problem.

Well-structured knowledge base

This ties in with the issue of motivation. Our experience is that students (and staff) need to have a clear idea that induction week is part of their formal course timetable. Students (and staff) also need to understand how each piece builds upon what they already know and how it will help them with what is to come. Unfortunately, when our students were given too much detail in the programme, they adopted a 'pick and mix' approach. This undermined the programme and created a bad impression for newcomers. Where they received a 'tight' programme that simply gave them time and place, attendance was much better.

Our experience also suggests that organizers of induction programmes need to engage in meticulous planning backed up by thorough contingency planning. If it can go wrong, then it probably will, particularly if it involves room booking and technology. The following thoughts may help you to avoid some of the pitfalls:

- involve students in planning prior to them going down in the summer. Involving students gets you other information to help you develop student-friendly procedures;

- check how your induction fits in with the rest of the department, particularly in regard to rooms and staffing;

- do not over assess; marking turn-around can be a problem;

- organize a budget for buffet, prizes, etc;

- induction programmes require a heavy course-leader input, so make sure that you are not expected to be doing anything else as well;

- evaluate what you do to aid continuous improvement.

To conclude, we would suggest that it is possible to teach these 'old dogs' new tricks, as long as they find it enjoyable.

REFERENCES

Beckwith, J B (1991) 'Approaches to learning, their context and relationship to assessment performance', *Higher Education*, 22, 17–30.

Ely, M G (1992) 'Differential adoption of study approaches within individual students', *Higher Education*, 23, 231–54.

Gibbs, G (1992) *Improving the Quality of Student Learning*, Technical and Educational Services Ltd.

Gow, L and Kember, D (1990) 'Does higher education promote independent learning?', *Higher Education*, 19, 307–22.

Heathcote, G, *et al.* (1988) *Curriculum Styles and Strategies*, FEU, London.

Entwistle, N J and Ramsden, P (1983) *Understanding Student Learning*, Croom Helm, Beckenham.

Richardson, J T E (1990) 'Reliability and replicability of the approaches to studying questionnaire', *Studies in Higher Education*, 15, 2.

Appendix 1: Results of the 1993 Level 2 Induction Evaluation Questionnaire

Question	Strongly agree	Agree	Neither agree or disagree	Disagree	Strongly disagree
I believe that it is important to have an induction course for the BA Business degrees	8%	56%	19%	15%	2%
The induction course was well organized	2%	54%	25%	17%	2%
The student services session was useful		32%	45%	15%	8%
A library tour was not needed	3%	49%	13%	35%	
The staff input on the use of the library for research was useful		17%	20%	59%	4%
The research topics were poorly chosen		27%	32%	38%	3%
The session on note-taking was worthwhile	4%	30%	48%	16%	2%
The use of tutor-selected small groups was a good idea		9%	14%	75%	2%
We do need tutor input on precis writing	2%	38%	29%	27%	4%
The use of Belbin preferences was helpful for group information		26%	21%	48%	5%
I still do not know how to use assessment criteria when preparing assignments		12%	28%	57%	3%
I enjoy being involved in peer assessment		1%	49%	48%	2%
After the induction course I feel better prepared for undergraduate study	8%	22%	37%	29%	4%

Appendix 2: Results of the 1994 Level 2 Induction Evaluation Questionnaire

Question	Strongly agree	Agree	Neither agree or disagree	Disagree	Strongly disagree
I did not see the point of the 'treasure hunt' group exercise	10	5	2	6	0
Providing afternoon tea was not necessary	5	7	5	5	1
The student services session was useful	0	9	10	4	0
A library tour was not needed	6	7	2	5	3
The staff input on the use of the library for research was useful	1	14	4	4	0
The paper titles were poorly chosen	3	4	11	5	0
The preparation of an academic paper was a worthwhile experience	3	11	7	2	0
The mixing of degree cohorts was unhelpful	1	4	10	8	0
We do need tutor input on note-taking	2	9	3	8	0
The session on placements and sponsorships was helpful	0	9	10	3	1
The session on writing analytically was helpful	1	11	5	6	0
I still do not know how to use assessment criteria when preparing assignments	1	3	5	13	0
The induction course was well organized	1	7	10	3	2
After the induction course I feel better prepared for undergraduate study	2	6	9	6	0

(Sample size 23%)

Appendix 3: Results of the 1994 Level 3 Induction Evaluation Questionnaire

Question	Strongly agree	Agree	Neither agree or disagree	Disagree	Strongly disagree
The project session helped me	0	8	5	6	5
The careers/postgraduate advice session was useful	3	13	8	0	0
Visiting speakers benefit the induction programme	3	8	10	3	0
Self-managed time was a useful inclusion in the programme	3	8	11	2	0
Staff input on the use of the library for research was useful	0	2	17	3	2
The induction course was well organized	0	6	10	7	1
It is essential to have an induction course	2	8	4	10	0
After the induction course I feel better prepared for my final year	0	1	7	12	4

(Sample size 24%)

Chapter 9

Supplemental Instruction:
Helping Students to Help Each Other

Deanna C Martin and F Kim Wilcox

SUPPLEMENTAL INSTRUCTION AND ACADEMIC SUPPORT

Recent discussion about educational reform has addressed accountability, quality assurance and cost-effectiveness. These high-profile, big-ticket items were not the inventions of HE. Instead, they emerged historically from late-night meetings of corporate executives seeking the competitive edge in the market place. As these issues gain relevancy for tertiary education, those of us in the academy find ourselves reevaluating many of our previously unquestioned assumptions, including what we mean by a quality education, and for whom. At issue in the present chapter is the manner of providing academic support for all students, including non-traditional students. The specific mechanism for support which this chapter considers, supplemental instruction, originated and developed on the campus of the University of Missouri in Kansas City (UMKC).

SUPPLEMENTAL INSTRUCTION AT THE UNIVERSITY OF MISSOURI, KANSAS CITY, USA

Supplemental instruction (SI), a non-traditional academic assistance programme, originated in 1973. Eight years later, after a rigorous review process, the SI programme became one of two in the post-secondary field to be designated by the US Department of Education as an 'Exemplary Educational Programme', a distinction that remains some 13 years later. The National Diffusion Network, the national dissemination agency for the US Department of Education, has made it possible for UMKC to disseminate SI to hundreds of institutions across the US. Staff from nearly 500 institutions from the US and abroad have been trained to implement SI.

Programme description

The programme was called 'supplemental instruction' because it features peer review sessions which 'supplement' the instruction that students receive. SI targets historically-difficult academic subjects and offers regularly scheduled out-of-class, peer-facilitated review sessions to all enrolled students. The SI sessions resemble informal seminars in which students integrate subject content and study strategies. The SI sessions are directed by 'SI leaders', usually students who have previously completed the 'high-risk' subject with high marks. Since attendance at SI is voluntary and no effort is made to segregate students based on academic ability, SI is not viewed by either staff or students as remedial.

In the traditional US model, SI leaders attend class lectures, take notes, read all assigned materials and convene three to five small group study sessions per week. SI leaders assume the role of the 'model student'. They receive training and supervision in group facilitation, proactive learning and study strategies.

In the UK as in the US, the traditional model varies to fit institutional and local needs. For example, in the UK it is difficult to schedule more than one or two hours of SI a week because of space and scheduling conflicts; therefore, many programmes train multiple SI leaders who convene sessions concurrently. Additionally, many faculties schedule lectures for both their first- and second-year students during the same hours, making impossible the attendance of second-year students at first-year lectures. This circumstance has led to closer ties between lecturer, tutor and SI leader as the latter seeks to confirm what the instructional team has presented and which concepts the lecturers and tutors view as 'primary'.

While the instructional staff provide all the content for the SI, student participants take all responsibility for the content discussion. The SI leader helps the group identify the topics they want to discuss. Together, SI participants discover appropriate study strategies as they struggle to understand the material by comparing notes, organizing data, working problems, developing questions, acquiring vocabulary and preparing for examinations. SI integrates how-to-learn with what-to-learn, using the material of the discipline as a vehicle for skill instruction. Research studies over the past decade from 146 US institutions (2,875 college subjects) document the following benefits for SI attenders: higher subject grades (one-half to one full letter grade), lower percentage of course withdrawals (one-quarter to one-half), higher semester enrolment rates, and higher graduation rates. Although evaluation data for US and UK programmes have dissimilar aspects,

> the SI programme, adapted for the British Higher Education system demonstrates that despite comparable entry qualifications and pre-SI performance, those who attend SI do significantly better on average than those who do not ... there is also some evidence that the rate of attrition improves (Rust and Wallace, 1994).

SI supervision

To be effective, SI must be supervised. Overall day-to-day responsibilities reside with the SI supervisor, usually a full-time professional who is trained in all aspects of the SI programme. The SI supervisor's duties require that person to identify the difficult subjects, to gain departmental cooperation for the use of SI, to select and train SI leaders, and to monitor the quality of the individual SI sessions. As the programme grows, the SI supervisor may be assisted by part-time personnel who are hired to assist with supervision, data collection and other tasks. It is important that the SI supervisor reports the results of the programme to upper-level management, including deans and directors, as well as key personnel within the office of the Vice-Chancellor. Successful programmes that go unreported soon go unfunded. SI personnel should consider reporting results that address the mission of the institution as well as the success of individual students in individual subjects.

Institutional benefits

SI supports high standards. Where growing numbers of students are academically under-prepared, SI offers the institution a cost-efficient and educationally effective programme designed to retain and enable the graduate students while protecting the academic integrity and rigour of the subject. SI focuses on reducing attrition while raising the general level of student performance to meet departmental standards.

SI enhances without duplicating the classroom experience. SI does not attempt to replace the role of the content expert by relecturing. Instead, SI utilizes the institution's most overlooked resource: the time students spend studying. As students interact with an experienced learner, they improve their ability to think independently and critically about academic issues as the content unfolds. Among the most widely recognized benefits of small-group, collaborative learning are that students understand more, remember longer, and use information with greater facility (Johnson, Johnson and Smith, 1991). Advocates of SI argue that their system both captures and manages the students' study time.

Evaluation is rigorous. Evaluation measures student performance rather than more subjective factors such as student and staff perceptions of the service. Because evaluation includes student grades, attrition and graduation rates, programme administrators can make informed decisions about cost-effective and educational benefits.

Student benefits

SI is proactive and participatory rather than reactive and passive. While engaged in answering each other's questions, students are in fact, *engaged.* Students need the opportunity to process information in a way that helps them make their own connections and, in so doing, solidify their understanding of the content. Engagement, in this case, is not the result of an artificial or contrived attempt to involve students in critical thinking activities; rather, it is the natural outcome of students investing in their own understanding.

SI promotes student assimilation into the academic culture of the campus. A personal sense of belonging to other individuals or groups on a campus stands out as an important factor in retention (Gardner and Jewler, 1992). First-year students are among the most likely to experience feelings of isolation and alienation (Tinto, 1987). This is especially true on large urban campuses where opportunities to share common experiences may be limited. On many campuses social activities are promoted with the hope that they will ultimately contribute to the academic structure. Student involvement in SI, however, is an academic activity that nurtures the social structure of the campus.

SI enjoys a non-remedial image while offering academic support to all students enrolled on historically-difficult subjects. Studies indicate there is a commensurate representation of students who attend SI sessions with respect to academic abilities, ethnicities, and gender (Martin and Arendale, 1991). In SI, similarities are emphasized and differences minimized as students share in the common cause of earning their subject marks.

SI provides the opportunity for SI leaders to develop leadership skills as they improve their own level of content competency in the subject areas. Both SI leaders and participating students benefit from processing and reviewing subject material. As SI leaders organize and direct group discussions, they have the opportunity to develop other transferable skills including those abilities related to leadership, problem-solving, public speaking, listening/communication and guidance and support (Rust and Wallace, 1994).

EFFECTIVENESS

SI, a structured field-based programme, offers a fully designed training component. Hundreds of institutions have adapted SI to meet the individual needs of their campuses. SI functions within the unique cultural environment of the institution, rather than as something superimposed. Over the last two decades, researchers and practitioners have produced evidence that strongly suggests that SI increases students' retention and performance in high risk subjects (see, for example, Burmeister, 1995). Many other factors have been studied that might account for the differences in performance and retention data; however, none has been shown to account for the positive effect (Martin and Arendale, 1991).

TROUBLESHOOTING SI

While training opportunities, technical assistance and advice abound, SI practitioners report areas of vulnerability in the model. Frequently, problems focus on areas of misunderstanding among administrators and staff. The most common problems divide along authority lines, specifically, who claims responsibility for the programme and whether its implementers include or exclude other university stakeholders. If SI is perceived, for example, as a 'top-down' programme imposed by the administration, staff are likely to view it as intrusive. If staff do not see the service as appropriate, they will inevitably communicate their impressions to students who, in turn, will not value SI if their lecturers and tutors fail to do so. Participation, therefore, will be low and the programme will not be cost-effective.

We strongly recommend that enthusiastic administrators introduce the programme by identifying well-respected staff who are willing to pilot SI in difficult subject areas. Providing implementation funds and adopting a hands-off approach are likely to yield the most positive results. More often, SI is introduced by a staff member or department chair who has been searching for some way to assist students. While grass-roots support remains essential, it is not sufficient to guarantee programme success. If upper administration do not understand and value the programme, they will not fund it, choosing instead to place all the burden for long-term funding on the department. Early discussions with top officials, therefore, can assure that if SI meets its goals and objectives, the university will invest in its continuation. Data collection and analysis, then, are key features of all successful programmes. SI often crosses traditional barriers of organizational structure to strengthen relationships among students, staff and administrators. By opening channels for meaningful interaction, various academic constituencies discover new opportunities to work together in support of student learning. Additionally, by mobilizing students to help one another, the institution captures an otherwise dormant resource within the academy.

REFERENCES

Burmeister, S (1995) 'Analysis of effectiveness of SI sessions for college algebra, calculus, and statistics', *Research in Collegiate Mathematics Education.*

Gardner, J and Jewler, A (1992) *Your College Experience: Strategies for success*, Belmont, CA: Wordsworth Publishing Company.

Johnson, D W, Johnson, R and Smith, K A (1991) 'Cooperative learning. Increasing college faculty instructional productivity', *AAHE-ERIC Higher Education Report No. 4*, Washington DC, The George Washington University, School of Education and Human Development.

Martin, D C and Arendale, D R (1991) 'Supplemental instruction: improving student performance, increasing student persistence', ERIC Document Reproduction Service, ED 327 103, 14 pp, MFOl, PCOl.

Rust, C and Wallace, J (eds) (1994) *Helping Students To Learn from Each Other*, Paper 86, Birmingham, UK, SEDA Publications.

Tinto, V (1987) *Leaving College: Rethinking the causes and cures of student attrition*, Chicago, IL: University of Chicago Press.

Chapter 10

Encouraging Students:
Making the Passive Active at the
Nottingham Trent University

Ian Solomonides and Malcolm Swannell

INTRODUCTION

Students starting analytical degrees in this and many other universities are displaying a series of dysfunctional learning strategies. Staff are reporting that, at worst, some students are inclined to adopt a passive, instrumental, surface or even apathetic approach to study and it is believed that a consequence is often a high attrition rate, low levels of interaction, and low levels of understanding. Espoused approaches to study theory suggest that appropriate deep and surface approaches are gateways to academic success or failure; this chapter suggests that it is the strategic and apathetic approaches that are most influential in student success, failure and level of engagement.

Learning to learn (LTL) workshops, computer-based study support, peer evaluation of staff and other curriculum interventions have been developed and/or supported by the authors at the Nottingham Trent University which our research suggests can help reorientate some students as well as identify and support those at risk of failing.

'Approach to study', the way in which students perceive, engage with and learn about their chosen fields of study is now commonly used to portray the quality of learning the student achieves. Approach to study and its part in a more general notion of the way in which students may 'orientate' themselves towards their study, is concerned with how and why students interact with the learning tasks they undertake. Descriptions of approach to study and orientation are reported (Biggs, 1976; Entwistle and Ramsden, 1983; Meyer, 1991) at conceptual and empirical levels to varying degrees of consensus. All approaches and orientations are at least partly context-dependent (many authors give the impression they are wholly dependent on the context in which the student operates).

The meaning-orientation approach describes a learning strategy involving a desire by the student to reach full understanding and develop personally a deep approach to study. Deep study implies that reaching a deep level of conceptual understanding is the intrinsic motivational goal. Information is thereby examined to identify the underlying concepts and meanings.

The achieving-orientation approach is a highly strategic mode involving a strategic approach to study where the student is determined to do well. Here, the mercenary application of effort respective to the implied desires of lecturers and assessments will result in success.

The reproducing-orientation approach is instrumental in character; it involves the superficial collection of knowledge and a surface approach to study which is shallow in nature and implies the use of rote learning and routine as a substitute for understanding. To pass assessments students will reproduce ideas and facts presented to them at an earlier date. The motive is to get extrinsic reward.

These approaches and orientations can be identified using questionnaires such as the Revised Approach to Study Inventory (RASI) developed by Entwistle and Tait (1992).

At Nottingham Trent, teaching staff are recognizing that students approach their studies in qualitatively different ways and that the incoming cohorts are quite diverse in apparent abilities and predispositions. Moreover, the type of learning we were trying to encourage was proving to be ineffective. One tutor, describing highly independent, self teaching, 'reading for a degree' type activity, remarked:

> This kind of learning is fine for the best students but we don't get them. Our students are learning that if they can get as much as possible out of the lecturer about what is in the exam they can learn just enough to pass. We are turning out students who actually represent low value for money... they simply don't understand the material.

So while we subscribe to the idea of 'improving student learning' and are prepared to describe and develop improvements in approach to study terms, in our context some very serious issues and problems are evident.

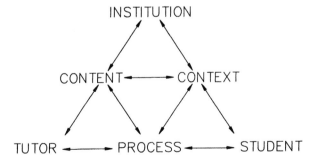

Figure 10.1 *Interacting elements of the learning and teaching system*

All HE, not just engineering, should be seen as a system where all the factors relate towards the quality of the learning outcome. As such, teaching and learning in HE will behave in a systemic way. This interrelationship of factors is represented in Figure 10.1. Here the institution, the tutor and the student act as a triad, each responding to the other. Between them lie the content, context and process of learning which are viewed or perceived uniquely by each member of the triad. Change to the system has an unpredictable effect and is unlikely to take place if only one of the elements in the system is altered, because it will return to the status quo under pressure from the rest of the system. For this reason, we know that if we wish to improve the quality of our students' learning, we have to intervene and influence at least two of the elements within the system. The rest of this chapter describes five inputs which are acting on at least three elements of the system.

INTERVENTIONS AT THE NOTTINGHAM TRENT UNIVERSITY

Learning to learn workshops

An initial system development was the deployment of a 'Learning skills facilitator' (Ian Solomonides). In attempting to make students more active, it was believed that maximum impact would be achieved by raising students' awareness of their study processes. Consequently a series of LTL workshops for students was developed. These encouraged incoming students to explore the notion of approach to study, with the aim of developing an appropriate orientation to future learning tasks. At the time, we believed it was most appropriate to aim to develop the meaning-orientation and the deep, more active approach to study. The workshops involved a total of eight student contact hours (four in the first term and four in the second), during which students were exposed to a series of exercises of the type found in many published sources (eg, Gibbs, 1982) and undertook a compulsory terminal essay asking them to reflect on their approaches to study and the implications thereafter for their course of study. Essentially, the LTL workshops acquired the status of discussion groups comprising as much philosophical discussion driven by the students as practical and theoretical input from the facilitator. The official programme of study for the LTL workshops included:

- reflecting on past experiences;
- describing approach to study;
- describing conceptions of learning;
- discussion of how to show quality in learning;
- memory and learning activities;
- organization;

- self-evaluation;

- reflection.

The workshops, trialed within the Integrated Engineering degree with a cohort of 53 first-year students, were well received, with students anecdotally reporting an increased awareness of their study disposition, for example:

> My learning method has changed a little without knowing why initially, but having read items I now understand my previous and current strategies and am now able to work on them. I could have done with this four years ago.

Was this level of enthusiasm and change to be reported by the Revised Approach to Study Inventory? Six months after the LTL workshops, this cohort of students provided profiles that revealed a general significant decrease in deep approach and a general significant increase in surface, strategic and apathetic approaches. This shift was also generally reported across all courses and students studied (n = 613). It would have seemed that the workshops had failed to achieve their aim, had it not been for the change reported by a small sub-group of Integrated Engineering students.

This sub-group comprised students at risk of failing as well as students appearing overly-anxious about studies and the implications of failing. Each of these students was further supported using one-to-one study counselling regarding concerns such as procrastination, fear-of-failure, and lack of direction and focus during their first year of study. It is assumed by staff and students involved that the at-risk students would have otherwise failed and that the overly-anxious would have performed with less efficacy.

It was concluded that the LTL workshops in their current form could not directly develop the approach to study of our engineering undergraduates. However, it was clear that the workshops were engaging students in the examination of their approaches to study and that students were more aware of their role in the teaching and learning processes as a result. Likewise the workshops had offered students a focus for any concern they wished to examine further and enabled some students to pursue their concern in a supportive and friendly atmosphere.

Computer-based study support

Alongside the LTL workshops, we were interested in developing a form of computer-based study support; something that would address some of the issues explicit in the workshops as well as issues we felt were legitimate concerns. These concerns were largely to do with the fragmented view students had of the interactive nature of the course.

We knew that students inclined to think of the course as providing ready-made chunks of information to be remembered in a passive way were likely to be less successful. The way in which the engineering curriculum is organized, especially within a modular system, gives the impression that the knowledge content is bundled discretely and is to be approached in that way. As well as information parallel to that contained in the LTL workshops, our 'integrated course map' (see Figure 10.2) therefore contained a chart and guide to the Integrated Engineering degree course content, learning outcomes and assessment procedures.

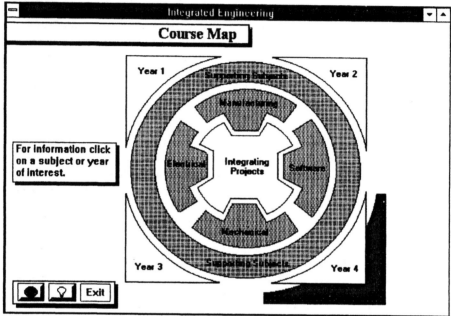

Figure 10.2   *Integrated course map: main menu*

The package, authored using Asymetrix Toolbook in Windows on the PC, is locally networked within the department. All information is accessed through a front screen and main menu giving a schematic representation of the course. From this main screen the student traverses through various levels of information as required.

Of course, this type of information is freely available in traditional course handbooks but, in that format, is often neglected and ignored. The integrated course map offers similar information in a way that is much more accessible to students now culturally familiar with accessing information on screen. In addition, the student can move into a section of the map that takes them through a series of exercises designed to force reflection on their approach and general attitude to study. No explicit study skills advice is given and we prefer to describe the content of this package as 'study strategies' information.

The study strategies section takes about 20 minutes of student time. The rest of the package can be accessed for as long as needed. Our logging of student use suggests that the package is regularly used; a short feedback questionnaire at the end of the study strategies section suggests students do find the package useful in gaining information about potential learning strategies and in promoting some personal reflection. The package subsequently won the Royal Mail-sponsored 1994 Partnership Trust award for the application of technology to the education of engineers.

The workshops and the computer support were clearly interventions aimed at the student part of the system. The workshops and research into teaching and learning gained wider acceptance within the department. This and external factors such as accreditation and quality audits led to a more general awareness on the part of teaching staff of the need to address explicitly issues of quality in teaching and learning. For the first time in the history of the department, the entire teaching staff met with an agenda to identify and prioritize objectives for the improvement of the teaching and learning milieu. From this meeting, four main areas were identified: peer evaluation of teaching, student feedback systems, workload and assessment mechanisms and teaching and learning research. We would argue that these all impact on the teaching and learning system shown in Figure 10.1 and, as stated earlier, are at least in part instrumental in improving the overall teaching and learning milieu. What now follows is a discussion of our experiences related to these areas and the impact they have had on promoting a more active approach to both learning *and* teaching.

PEER EVALUATION OF TEACHING

Peer evaluation, in which colleagues sit in on lectures and seminars, provides feedback to individual lecturers on style, content and appropriateness of their teaching. It is the intention that this be carried out in as 'non-threatening' a manner as possible. Peer evaluation aims to improve the quality of interaction between tutor and student. Good practice in developing methods to encourage students to become more active can be identified and this practice disseminated within the department and the institution.

The mechanism for this process is initially based on voluntary commitment to the practice and principle of peer observation. A principal lecturer, having experience in classroom observation at a number of different engineering establishments, was given the responsibility of introducing the initiative into our department. Three other lecturers and the learning skills facilitator expressed an interest and were enlisted to assist in the development of the process and to carry out the observations. Both authors form part of this team. As part of the 'ground rules' it was agreed by this group that two observers be involved and that the observed have the opportunity to indicate their preference for lectures, seminars, workshops or other type of delivery. Individual lecturers are also given the right to veto the choice of observers. The intention is to reinforce the view that peer observation is aimed at developing teaching as well as informing good practice in teaching and learning.

The mechanism of peer observation was initially promoted on a voluntary basis. Tutors wishing to receive feedback on their teaching first identified themselves to the principal lecturer referred to above. This initial group was then observed at some stage during the first semester of 1994/95. This has now developed so that there is a further requirement that all other full-time academic staff within the department are observed in the second semester of the same academic year. While it is recognized that observing staff from other departments who service our courses would be desirable, it was felt that the observers did not have the necessary authority in this matter. However, the observing group agree that once the appropriate skills and experience have been gained, then its services could be offered on a consultancy basis to other courses both within our own university and at other educational establishments.

The peer observation practice involves two colleagues observing a delivery. Both observers are members of a small group from within the department, chosen for their acknowledged expertise in teaching (as anecdotally reported by their peers) and their knowledge of the subject area concerned. Initial criteria for evaluation are those used and published by the HEFCE. Whenever possible, immediate verbal feedback is given to the lecturer in an open discussion of the strengths and weaknesses of the session. After a period of reflection, the two observers provide a fuller written report in which the views of the observed lecturer are encouraged. An anonymous executive summary of this report is provided to the observing team leader in order to attempt to establish traits and trends that are common across the department. This also provides a valued mechanism to disseminate good practice as well as to highlight the importance of teaching and learning in our department and to promote further debate on educational issues.

The emphasis of peer evaluation is on encouraging good teaching practice. As such the main outcomes of the process are considered to be:

- improvement in individual delivery through feedback and sharing of good practice;

- raising of the awareness of engineering education issues through discussion;

- promotion of the importance of teaching and learning within the department;

- development of a team attitude, instead of a closed-door approach to teaching;

- highlighting and sharing of common problems in the teaching of our students;

- provision of implicit messages to students about staff interest in teaching quality.

Furthermore, acting as a development process the observations will identify staff *and student* training needs and prove to be as beneficial to the observers as to the observed. The peer evaluation has proved to be very useful indeed. No negative feedback about its purpose has been received from any of the observed or the observers. Despite initial concern about if and how observation would be linked to appraisal, the scheme has now established itself as a tool of staff development, 'sold to' its users as a way of developing professional practice.

The scheme is in effect quite low-key and exists because of the personalities involved in its development and because tutors accept that they are in future likely to be examined by external bodies. It also marks the recognition our departmental staff have of the links between good teaching and high quality learning. This is one of the benefits of researching into teaching and learning at a local level. Both authors have for some time been examining various aspects of undergraduate learning. This has led directly to a change in culture within the department, whereby staff and students are far more willing and keen to discuss their teaching and learning, to examine their conceptions and misconceptions than they were before.

STUDENT FEEDBACK

While student feedback has always been obtained both formally and informally, the systems employed have sometimes been aimless in nature and resulted in criticism of isolated problems and issues, rather than providing a constructive dialogue about major course issues. The importance of this type of feedback is recognized; however, the department feels that it is also necessary to obtain feedback on more strategic course matters. A number of initiatives have been introduced to attempt to increase the effectiveness of student feedback. One such practice is discussed below.

In addition to established procedures, one of the authors (Malcolm Swannell) introduced a more structured process of student feedback. This involved the distribution of two questionnaires to final year Integrated Engineering students. The first of these was the RASI. This was used to obtain information about student study methods in order to assess the overall effect of studying engineering on student strategies. The second was the Course Experience Questionnaire (CEQ) (Ramsden, 1991), which was used to obtain a measure of the effectiveness of the course in developing some of the qualities valued in HE.

As an important adjunct to the CEQ, students were invited to comment on the following points:

- individual subjects and course organization;
- workload;
- project management;
- computer resources;
- library facilities;
- general comments.

An analysis of the questionnaires and, in particular, the additional comments, provided a valuable agenda for a follow-up meeting with all of the final-year students on the course. As it was held with final-year students towards the end of the year, it encouraged valuable feedback in a balanced manner of the whole of the course. It further proved a means of concentrating student minds on strategic course issues that are considered important by the course management team, as well as the students who had ownership of the agenda.

ASSESSMENT AND WORKLOAD

An issue recognized as being important by academic staff is that of workload. It is felt by staff that engineering has a large knowledge base and as a consequence the students have a heavy taught workload when compared to many other disciplines. It is acknowledged by some, but not all staff, that this workload is prohibitively high and that students do not always have time to think in a manner appropriate to HE. While this concern has been partially addressed in the department, there is emerging opinion that assessment has a critical role in driving student workload. It is recognized that the type of assessment will often govern approaches to study, in that an assessment that relies upon the recall of fact will often evoke a surface approach, whereas an assignment requiring research of, and critical comment on, subject matter should evoke a deeper approach (Brown and Knight, 1994). A strategic response to a heavy workload will also often result in students taking a less desirable approach to study in order to survive the course.

The Academic Development Committee for the department regularly investigates assessment with a view to containing failure at a reasonable rate. This committee also has a wider remit to investigate the effects of workload. We believe that this is one of the more important issues to be addressed in engineering education. In support of this view, Vos (1991) presents information on the relationship of study time and contact time as well as the effect of assessment on study habits. Figures 10.3 and 10.4 illustrate the concept of assessment and workload. The Figure 10.3 pattern uses phase tests regularly throughout the year. In this model, students develop the habit of postponing independent study until the period immediately prior to the next test. Independent study is only generated by coursework and students rely upon cramming to pass. Figure 10.3 therefore represents:

- one hour of lectures per week;
- three in-course tests and one final examination;
- assessment-driven learning;
- students postponing independent study as they cram for tests;
- independent study being governed by coursework alone.

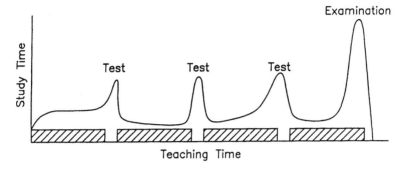

Figure 10.3 *In course tests and final examination*

The model shown as Figure 10.4 assumes a final examination with an emphasis on lectures and seminars, for which students have to prepare well. Lectures become the main source of information and are delivered in a manner that forces preparation, so that this becomes a focus of the learning process. In this instance, it is suggested that learning is more evenly spread throughout the year and that a greater level of independent study is generated. The best preparation starts on the first day of the academic year and not two to three weeks before the examination.

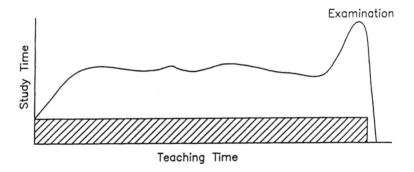

Figure 10.4 *Final examination with learning emphasis*

Figure 10.4 represents:

● two hours of lectures per week;

● no intermediate tests;

● students preparing well for lectures and seminars;

● lectures focused and targeted on the learning process;

- lectures as a main source of information;
- students aware of their responsibilities.

There is therefore merit in this second model. It is not suggested that a final examination be used as the only form of assessment. Assignments, projects, laboratory work and design all have an important role in developing study and other personal skills. However, the course team must carefully consider the level, frequency and timing of continuously assessed work in order to avoid the problems inherent in Figure 10.3.

RESEARCH AT THE NOTTINGHAM TRENT UNIVERSITY

We have also been conducting research into the approach to study of our engineering undergraduates using the RASI. Initially, we collected study profiles for all students entering engineering and computing degrees in the academic year 1992/93. Factor analysis revealed the existence of four main factors:

- a reproducing-orientation factor;
- a meaning-orientation factor;
- an achieving-orientation factor;
- an apathetic-orientation factor.

These constructs of orientation were then used as an index against which future work could be developed and any claims for changes in approach to study substantiated.

As successive cohorts of students progressed to the end of the year, we found that their assessment performance was associated with two of the above factors. A good assessment outcome was found to correlate most strongly with the achieving-orientation factor and a poor assessment outcome was found to correlate most strongly with the apathetic-orientation factor. Conceptually and empirically there is little evidence for the apathetic-orientation existing totally separately. It is far more likely that the apathetic-orientation is a reversed achieving-orientation. This means that in our context, student success was most closely tied to strategic/apathetic dispositions rather than deep/surface dispositions as suggested by espoused approach theories. We do, of course, recognize the pivotal effect elements like workload and assessment have on orientation and approach to study, and that the adoption of an achieving-orientation by our students may be a reaction to these elements. However, we argue that the approach to study epistemology may be incomplete and does not adequately describe the most beneficial approach to learning within disciplines such as engineering.

Students likely to do well and succeed within engineering are those who have study orientations associated with an achieving-orientation and the reverse of the apathetic-orientation. For us, this positive strategic approach goes beyond the constructs given earlier and begins to suggest that notions of deep, active learning can be seen as a more energetic form of surface learning as engineering students charge off in the pursuit of depth without realizing the essential need for strategic, compromising abilities. In our construct, strategic learning involves critically thinking about the task in hand to offer a careful and deliberated response. Having a strategic disposition is all about choice: being able to choose the best or the most appropriate response for the application and context in question; what might be described in engineering terms as 'optimizing constraints'.

Students who do well on our courses are those who optimize the constraints and balance the resources they have to work with. They strategically go about learning engineering from the context they engage with. Those who fail do the opposite of this. In terms of helping students deal with their immediate surroundings and situation, the deep and surface approaches are second order; we have to address the need to get our students dealing strategically with time, the content *and* their thinking first. Previously our intervention efforts have been targeted at evoking deeper approaches and meaning-orientations. Following our research, we are now considering redirecting our efforts in favour of an approach and orientation most suited to our discipline and context. Within the limits of the present descriptions these are the strategic approach to study and achieving-orientation.

CONCLUSIONS

In writing this chapter we have taken an eclectic look at some of the innovations in which we have been involved. In doing so, we wanted to allude to the interrelationship between these various activities and their impact. The notion of a system referred to at the beginning of this chapter indicates how changes within the system can never be driven by one input at one time. Many practitioners fail to recognize the highly interdependent cultural elements within such a system and therefore the length of time and effort needed to create change. Development in this context has to be driven by both staff and student needs.

The LTL workshops were specifically aimed at raising the awareness of student-study processes. The computer course map has been used by students to orientate themselves to the course, including integration of themes, study options and assessment requirements. The map also provides advice on study strategies. Peer evaluation of teaching provides a valuable means of identifying and disseminating practices that encourage tutor-student interaction. Assessment and workload have been identified as having a major impact on study strategies in engineering. We argue therefore, that these four elements, combined with research into teaching and learning at a local level, all have an impact on the teaching and learning system and can contribute positively towards the process of making students more active. These are the elements that we examined and that consequently had some effect on the attitudes of the teachers and the taught. We do not advocate that they are the elements that every practitioner should look at in every context. The implications we feel to be most relevant are that by involving ourselves at a local level and dealing with issues deemed to be important within our own department, we have changed what initially appeared to be an immutable system.

In particular, our experiences of developing and supporting teaching and learning interventions, some of which we have described here, lead us to suggest that:

- improving the quality of learning requires inputs to at least two elements of the teaching and learning system;

- leading interventions *in isolation* do not necessarily alter the approach to study of students; however, they have a valuable proactive role in identifying students 'at risk of failing';

- technology can be usefully applied to the support of student learning, particularly in the strategic-orientation of students towards the structure and requirements of a course;

- peer evaluation used as staff development will encourage excellence in teaching by improving individual delivery and disseminating good practice;

- using a structured approach to student feedback will provide valuable information about strategic course issues and the learning environment;

- assessment is critical in driving student workload and the level, frequency and timing of continuous assessment must be carefully balanced in order to avoid students taking a surface approach to survive the course;

- engineers need to 'optimize constraints'. Students do well on our courses by optimizing constraints in taking a strategic approach to study.

We have identified the above list of suggestions as effective only because the climate within the Department of Mechanical Engineering is such that staff and students are beginning to feel that they work within a culture that encourages teaching and learning. This type of culture is not typical within higher engineering education. It exists in our department because of a series of events, including the appointment of a locally-based student- and staff-development facilitator. Changes in attitude and culture develop very slowly and are still developing. From our experience we recommend that this change in culture is developed incrementally from a local base of interested and enthused colleagues. Our observations lead us to believe that, once established, the credibility of these types of interventions will pervade the department such as to alter the attitudes and opinions of even the most intransigent of staff.

REFERENCES

Biggs, J B (1976) 'Dimensions of study behaviour: another look at the ATT', *British Journal of Educational Psychology*, 46, 68–80.

Brown, S and Knight, P (1994) *Assessing Learning in Higher Education*, Kogan Page, London.

Entwistle, N and Ramsden, P (1983) *Understanding Student Learning*, Croom Helm, Beckenham.

Entwistle, N and Tait, H (1992) *The Revised Approach to Study Inventory*, The Centre for Research on Learning and Instruction, University of Edinburgh.

Gibbs, G (1982) *Teaching Students to Learn*, Open University Press, Buckingham.

Meyer, J H F (1991) 'Study orchestration: the manifestation, interpretation and consequences of contextualised approaches to studying', *Higher Education*, 22, 297–316.

Ramsden, P (1991) 'A performance indicator of teaching quality in higher education: the course experience questionnaire', *Studies in Higher Education*, 16/2, 129–50.

Vos, P (1991) 'Curriculum control of learning processes in higher education', *Proceedings of the 13th International Forum on Higher Education of the European Association for Institutional Research*, Edinburgh.

Chapter 11

Using Scaffolding to Enable Student Learning: A New Zealand Computer Programming Experience

John Waddick, Pamela Wood and Maxine Alterio

INTRODUCTION

Educators have a responsibility to create opportunities for students both to gain new knowledge and understanding and to augment their range of approaches to learning. When designing a programme, the educator can choose teaching strategies which enable students to learn the particular content of the course, as well as to increase their higher-level thinking skills.

This case study describes how a 12-hour computer programming module enabled students to refine their problem-solving strategies, extend their meta-cognitive skills (particularly planning, monitoring and reflection), increase their autonomy in learning, and explore cooperative ways of working with peers in a computing environment. The lecturer's role was to 'scaffold' three things: the introduction of computer programming techniques, the development of problem-solving strategies and metacognitive skills, and the degree of support necessary for students to take more responsibility for their own learning.

This module formed the introductory component of the computing section of a science and technology course at Otago Polytechnic, Dunedin, New Zealand. Using Hypercard Tn, the 15 students were required to design, create and evaluate a computer program that could be used to aid learning in any subject in their course and provide a resource for other students. These computing projects were evaluated using peer and lecturer assessment.

SCAFFOLDING

Scaffolding is a recognized teaching approach to develop students' higher-level cognitive skills (eg, Palincsar and Brown, 1984; Tobias, 1982; Wood *et al.*, 1976). Scaffolds are forms of support provided by the teacher (or another student) to help students bridge the gap between their current abilities and the intended

116

goal (Rosenshine and Meister, 1992:26). While scaffolds provide support for the student they do not specify every step in learning a new technique. They can be both temporary and adjustable depending on student requirements. As students become more proficient and their need for scaffolding decreases, the lecturer must judge when and how to withdraw the support.

In this study, one scaffolding technique was the structured introduction of small components of content-specific information. At the beginning of each teaching session, the lecturer provided a ten-minute demonstration of a specific programming technique including text-writing, diagram-drawing, interactive question-formation, picture display and the use of hypertext features. Students could then decide for themselves if they wanted to follow up on any of the techniques. This scaffolding approach was used in combination with individual access to the lecturer as a resource person.

As they became more engaged in their projects, the students and lecturer together decided to discontinue these introductory segments, an example of withdrawing scaffolding as it becomes redundant. Other scaffolding techniques used by the lecturer related more particularly to the development of problem-solving strategies and metacognitive skills.

Problem-solving strategies

Problem-solving processes were scaffolded through modelling by the lecturer in the early stages of the module. Again it was important for the lecturer to withdraw this scaffolding at the correct time to avoid frustrating students who were motivated to find their own pathways. Students could then individually approach the lecturer who would model problem solving using another scaffold, 'thinking aloud', when a student asked a complex question.

Students in this computing module were encouraged to use a range of problem-solving processes, as good problem solvers, according to Glaser (1992), are those who have a number of strategies available and know when to apply them. Students did, in fact, develop a variety of strategies including seeking feedback from peers, observing peers as they solved problems, and using resources such as textbooks and the open access computer suite which was available after hours. One innovative use of a resource involved students 'dismantling' a Hypercard tutorial package to examine how programming could be achieved.

Metacognitive skills

Metacognition relates to a person's ability to be aware of their thinking processes (Brown, 1987; Ryba and Anderson, 1990). Schwartz and Perkins maintain that well-designed instruction should encourage students to become metacognitive because this puts them in charge of their own thinking. Through reflection, they can probe and access, revise and test, their own thinking processes. This will promote further autonomous development of thinking beyond the range of the immediate instruction (1989:51).

This module focused on the development of the specific metacognitive skills of planning, monitoring and reflection.

Planning

Planning is recognized both as a metacognitive skill and as a significant step in the problem-solving process itself (Lawson, 1991; McKeachie, 1987). The need for planning was emphasized by the lecturer. Linn (1986) notes that while there is a resistance to planning within many problem-solving activities, in computer programming there is a greater acceptance of its integral role. This was not necessarily so in this case study. Although advised to, most students did not develop comprehensive plans on paper but started straight into their projects. This does not, however, preclude planning that might have occurred in other ways. Those that did make a written plan seemed also to be those who explored more complex and creative possibilities in their problem-solving. They were also the students who became more proficient in using reflective techniques.

Monitoring

From the beginning of the module, students were encouraged to monitor their progress in programming. The lecturer's role in helping students cultivate this metacognitive skill was to encourage them to experiment with various programming ideas and evaluate their effectiveness. This was particularly so when students asked specifically whether a particular programming script would work. By emphasizing the need for them to monitor and evaluate their own work, the lecturer helped students gain confidence in their ability to learn independently.

Reflection

Besides monitoring their progress in programming, students were also asked to reflect explicitly on their learning processes. To do this, they used a diary sheet developed by the lecturer. This was filled in at the end of each session and required only a few sentences for completion. Students were asked to record what they had done in the session, how they had changed their ideas, what sources of information they had used, the key events they considered important and what they would do about any problems identified. An example from one student illustrates their recognition of the importance of planning and the value of a specific strategy they had devised as part of their own planning and problem-solving approach:

> Before beginning I made a plan of what I wanted the program to do, and what I wanted to appear on the screen. So I really put myself in the position of the user rather than the programmer. I found this to be really helpful in working things out.

Students who made a written plan for their programme tended also to become more proficient in the use of their diary as the course progressed.

AUTONOMOUS LEARNING

In the use of any scaffolding technique the responsibility for learning gradually shifts from the lecturer to the student. Knowing when to withdraw the scaffold is crucial. Palincsar and Brown (1984) describe this shift in the lecturer's role as being from coach to supportive resource person. In doing so the lecturer encourages the student to become a more autonomous learner. As Higgs has noted:

> autonomous learning is a process in which the learner works on a learning task or activity and is largely independent of the teacher who acts as a manager of the learning programme and as a resource person (1988:40–41).

In this instance Higgs relates autonomous learning to the level of dependence on the teacher, recognizing that autonomy is relative rather than complete. Limitations imposed by the educational setting can be balanced by potential advantages, including the lecturer's facilitation, institutional resources and the stimulus and resources provided by other learners.

In this computing module, students were encouraged to exercise autonomy in their learning by being given control over deciding on a topic for their project, selecting their own resources and determining their own strategies for learning. Most students used the lecturer at first for guidance but decreased their dependence on him as they became more proficient in using textbooks as a main resource. Some students still preferred to consult the lecturer but also used peers as part of their learning process.

COOPERATIVE LEARNING IN A COMPUTING CONTEXT

Ryba and Anderson (1990) stress that when learners are problem solving in a computer environment it is important that the teacher provides a setting that is socially interactive and encourages reflection. The computing module was designed to provide ample opportunity for peer discussion. Although students were invited to work in pairs on their projects, this was strongly opposed by those who particularly wanted to work individually, as they did not want to be dependent on another person who might lose interest or be absent for some sessions. Only two decided to work as a pair. This to some extent mirrored the experience in other studies (eg, Nolte and Singer, 1985; Englert *et al.*, 1991) where the lecturers designed the courses so that students, after an initial cooperative learning experience, worked on individual projects. The difference with this computer programming module was that most students exercised the autonomy they had been given by choosing to work alone from the beginning.

Nevertheless, cooperative learning strategies were evident in other ways. Students consulted each other about specific aspects of programming and used the problem-solving mechanisms of their peers. One student said that testing his work out on peers helped him to develop his project for the user in a better way.

A further way they worked cooperatively was in the assessment of completed projects. In the final session students demonstrated the programs they had designed. They enjoyed this opportunity to share their successes. The programs were assessed by their peers and by the lecturer, with another lecturer acting as moderator, using a marking schedule devised by the students. This event was considered an important part of the course by all students who recognized the effort peers had made to complete their projects. Each student received a mark out of ten from each of their peers and from the lecturers, based on the fit between the student's intention with the programme and their successful achievement of this. There was little variation between the marks assigned for each student.

STUDENT REFLECTIONS: ROSEMARY AND SALLY

On completion of the module, all students commented that they had not only learned skills in computer programming but had also extended their problem-solving strategies. Two students were interviewed to gain a fuller understanding of these aspects of their learning.

Rosemary

Rosemary worked on her own to produce an interactive page of pictures that children could 'click on' to hear the sounds of animals and see some simple animations. She decided on this topic because she was interested in art, liked working with children and felt that city children had limited opportunity to interact with animals. While the short introductory scaffolding segments were important, they introduced more programming commands than she needed. Rosemary tended to use the lecturer as a resource during the timetabled session, while out of class time she requested assistance from a peer particularly skilled in programming. She increasingly used a textbook as the module progressed and was one of the students who 'dismantled' the tutorial program to examine programming options. In addition to this variety of problem-solving strategies, Rosemary chose to write out a plan for her project as she knew she would otherwise have no direction.

In assessing her project Rosemary considered that the graphics and sounds were good features. She expressed a real sense of achievement and was interested in developing the project further. As Rosemary reflected on her involvement in the module overall she commented that she had enjoyed the challenge and felt satisfied at producing something worthwhile.

Sally

Sally also worked individually to create a program of notes and diagrams of worms, as a study resource for part of a biology class she was taking. Sally disliked computers and thought this would be the easiest project to do. She took a long time to grasp the fundamentals of the task and found it took a lot of effort to complete the programming. For Sally, the autonomous nature of the module was not something she enjoyed. She preferred tasks where she 'just had to follow a set of instructions'. She found thinking up her own ideas 'quite difficult'.

When Sally began the project, she initially copied text from the tutorial programme, thinking this might help her solve programming problems. After the second week she decided this text did not provide the necessary support and that requesting help from a competent peer was a more effective way of obtaining the information she needed. Although this peer did recommend the use of a variety of other resources including textbooks, Sally still chose to abandon the use of texts.

Sally found it difficult to describe what was good about her project, despite it being as well developed as others in the class. The best she could say was that it was set out in a simple way for the user. She felt its main weakness was that it was not challenging enough and did not require much thinking on the user's part.

CONCLUSION

By choosing to use the teaching technique of scaffolding, the lecturer was able to introduce new knowledge about programming to the students as well as to develop their autonomy in learning, their problem-solving strategies and their metacognitive skills. Knowing when to withdraw the scaffolding was the key factor in ensuring its effectiveness. This was evident in his approach to the development of problem-solving skills. Initially he took a coaching role by modelling problem-solving processes. As this direct scaffolding was gradually withdrawn, the lecturer's role focused on encouraging creative experimentation and providing relevant resources. If he was engaged in modelling at all in the later stages of the module, it was more through thinking aloud when a student asked a complex question. By withdrawing direct scaffolding he was able to increase the students' level of autonomous learning.

In any group, students will need different degrees of support and structure in their learning. While Rosemary preferred limited structure and felt confident with the degree of autonomy in choosing her own learning strategies, Sally was more anxious in making these decisions for herself. She would have preferred a fully structured course, with limited learner autonomy. Nevertheless, she still followed her own strategies in learning, first in copying text from the tutorial program and then focusing on help from a competent peer.

Rosemary was a confident and autonomous learner from the outset. Sally, on the other hand, although hesitant and anxious at the beginning of the module, found ways to manage her own learning, though possibly still with a degree of dependence on others. The lecturer's original scaffolding of information and direct help, and the subsequent withdrawing of this, enabled both students to increase their autonomy as learners.

Although the lecturer had originally anticipated that students would work on collaborative projects, this option was chosen by only one pair. Students did, however, find other ways to work cooperatively which enhanced their learning and paradoxically their autonomy. By choosing to use each other as learning resources they increased their degree of independence from the lecturer. This also encouraged them to develop their own pathways to successful learning, including a new repertoire of problem-solving strategies. In the final session of the module, all students commented that their problem-solving skills had increased. Through deliberate fostering by the lecturer, the metacognitive skills of planning, monitoring and reflection were also successfully extended.

(Note: John Waddick is the lecturer involved in this case study. Rosemary and Sally are pseudonyms.)

REFERENCES

Brown, A (1987) 'Metacognition, executive control, self-regulation and other more mysterious mechanisms', in Weinert, F and Kluwe, R (eds) *Metacognition, Motivation and Understanding*, Erlbaum, Hillsdale, NJ.

Englert, C, Raphael, T, Anderson, L, Anthony, H and Stevens, D (1991) 'Making strategies and self-talk visible: writing instruction in regular and special education classrooms', *American Educational Research Journal*, 28: 337–72.

Glaser, R (1992) 'Learning, cognition and education: then and now', in Pick, H, van der Broek, P and Knill, D (eds) *Cognition: Conceptual and Methodological Issues*, American Psychological Association, Washington DC.

Higgs, J (1988) 'Planning learning experiences to promote autonomous learning', in Boud, D (ed.) *Developing Student Autonomy in Learning*, 2nd edn, Kogan Page, London.

Lawson, M (1991) 'Managing problem solving', in Biggs, J (ed.) *Teaching for Learning, the View from Cognitive Psychology*, Australian Council for Educational Research, Hawthorne, Victoria.

Linn, M (1986) 'Science', in Dillon, R and Sternberg, R (eds) *Cognition and Instruction*, Academic Press, Orlando.

McKeachie, W (1987) 'Cognitive skills and their transfer', *Journal of Educational Research*, 11, 6, 707–12.

Nolte, R and Singer, H (1985) 'Active comprehension: teaching a process of reading comprehension and its effects on reading achievement', *The Reading Teacher*, 39: 24–31.

Palincsar, A and Brown, A (1984) 'Reciprocal teaching of comprehension-fostering and comprehension-monitoring activities', *Cognition and Instruction*, 2: 117–75.

Rosenshine, B and Meister, C (1992) 'The use of scaffolds for teaching higher-level cognitive strategies', *Educational Leadership*, 49, 7, 26–33.

Ryba, K and Anderson, B (1990) *Learning with Computers: Effective Teaching Strategies*, ISTE, Eugene.

Schwartz, R and Perkins, D (1989) *Teaching Thinking: Issues and Approaches*, Hawker Brownlow, Australia.

Tobias, S (1982) 'When do instructional methods make a difference?', *Educational Researcher*, 11: 4–10.

Wood, D, Bruner, J and Ross, G (1976) 'The role of tutoring in problem solving', *Journal of Child Psychology and Psychiatry*, 17: 89–100.

Chapter 12

Designing a Computer-based Learning Application in the Biological Sciences

Erica J Morris and Mike A Tribe

INTRODUCTION

This chapter describes the design of BioActive: an application to support students taking the course 'Energy from biomass'. It provides a context to highlight issues that arise in the design of computer-based learning (CBL) in HE.

The design and implementation of BioActive is one part of a programme of computer-based activities currently under development within the School of Biological Sciences at Sussex. Tutorials have always been a key element in teaching and learning in this department since it started in 1961 and today the tutorial system is coming under considerable pressure for five main reasons:

- the educational background of students coming to university has changed (broadened) over the past ten years;

- the numbers of students has increased dramatically (more than doubled since 1980);

- the staff to student ratio has deteriorated;

- there are serious limitations on space;

- the conventional tutorial may not always be the most appropriate learning experience because it is normally tutor-led. We are therefore examining ways of providing cost-effective interactive learning facilities without the need for conventional tutorials. We are also conscious of the challenge to our graduates of obtaining jobs, both now and in the foreseeable future.

This means that the educational experience we provide for our undergraduates should not only be concerned with subject content and experimental design, important as these are, but also other skills. For example, we must help them develop sound communication skills, as well as flexibility in outlook, so that they can adapt to different and changing situations. Furthermore, we need to inculcate in them an ability to know where and how to obtain relevant information and not simply rely upon lectures or a few textbooks, so that they can critically appraise ideas for themselves, discuss issues with peers, and make informed opinions or sound decisions based upon them. To facilitate these skills, our aim has been to develop opportunities for interdependence in learning with small groups of third-year students, who are required to apply their knowledge and build interdisciplinary 'bridges' to the solution of real-life or simulated problems.

Fortunately, our thinking has coincided with funding from the Enterprise in Higher Education Initiative (EHEI), which has been encouraging departments to change their teaching methods so that they are more 'interactive' by, for example, the use of multimedia materials, computer-based learning and small group teaching and by placing a greater emphasis on student initiative in various forms (Entwistle, 1991). As a project, the development of BioActive is largely a response to the concerns of the EHEI. In addition, it is representative of the trend in HE towards the development, use and support of computer-based learning.

The purpose of this chapter is to address issues that arise in the development of computer-based courseware. These issues are raised in the context of the design of BioActive and illustrate that the design of CBL in HE is not a straightforward task. It is also important to emphasize that there is much (often implicit) excitement and enthusiasm concerning the use of CBL in HE (for example, Marsh and Kumar, 1992). It is recognized, however, that the simple use of computer-based courseware will not necessarily benefit, enhance, or facilitate student learning (Hammond, 1993; Laurillard, 1993; Shuell, 1992). Rather, developers and educators should not only strive to design and use systems that possess educational and instructional validity but must also clearly anticipate the context of their delivery (Laurillard, 1993; Shuell, 1992).

METHODOLOGY: USER-CENTRED DESIGN

A valuable approach for the effective and successful development of interactive software is user-centred design (Dix *et al.*, 1993; Preece, 1993). In this approach to system development, the users' needs are taken into account throughout the design process and testing and evaluation of the system with users is carried out to make sure that the system is designed to meet their needs. Accordingly, the design process is iterative where there are many cycles of 'design-test with users-redesign' (Preece, 1993, p.42). The requirements for an interactive system cannot be fully specified from the beginning of the life cycle and so the design (or aspects of the design) must be tested out with the end-users. The early prototypes can then be modified and improved in response to evaluation with users. This approach is seen as essential to the successful development of interactive software (Dix *et al.*, 1993) and many of its principles and methods can be adopted in the development of computer-based courseware. For example, it is recognized that courseware developers should carry out developmental testing and piloting of learning materials (Laurillard, 1993).

Against the above, the starting point in the design of BioActive was an initial requirements specification. This attempts to describe what the eventual system will be expected to provide and is not static but is refined and modified during the design process (Cox and Walker, 1993; Dix *et al.*, 1993). The completion of the requirements specification was valuable because it focused ideas and allowed us to identify the functions that BioActive should provide:

- *Multimedia*: the application will provide elements of text, graphics, sound, flow charts, photographic images, and video clips.

- *Activities and tasks to facilitate learning and/or problem solving*: the application will provide specific questions (on screen) to stimulate discussion and guide the students working as a pair. If appropriate, simulations, interactive and/or dynamic flowcharts and animations will be provided.

- *Additional facilities*:

    a map to illustrate the structure of the programme, and to indicate the possible programme paths that may be taken;
    an indication of the amount of material in each section of the programme to allow planning (see Laurillard, 1993);
    a set of learning objectives;
    a glossary;
    references (a) available for student consultation (b) consulted in the writing of the courseware;
    a study skills section concerning report writing and referencing (excerpt from requirements specification).

A user-centred approach in system development per se is insufficient in the design and development of CBL, because there are a number of other important activities and factors that must be considered and carried out in the development of learning materials. For example, the developers must decide what type of instructional system they are going to develop: a hypertext system, a multimedia resource, or a simulation program. Frequently, the subject area must also be structured and organized, and the optimal sequence for the learner may have to be determined. Accordingly, additional methods that guide the design of CBL must also be employed in system development. These methods provide guidelines and procedures which serve to assist the developers of computer-based courseware. The requirements of BioActive in the form of its functions outlined above were therefore mainly devised with reference to a method for courseware design (Laurillard, 1993). In addition, an approach to instructional design (Shuell, 1992) is also partly employed in the design of BioActive.

Prior to outlining the use of these two design methods, the general design of any computer-based courseware should look to what the computer can offer for student learning (that for example, the textbook, handout, video or lecturer, cannot). Shuell (1992) emphasizes that it is valuable to consider the advantages of using computers for instruction so that the unique features or possibilities of the computer can be harnessed and/or efforts can be made to capitalize on these advantages.

THE COMPUTER FOR LEARNING

There are at least three main areas where the developer can use the computer to advantage in delivering instruction. First, computers can present dynamic visual displays and/or graphics which are impossible with white board or handouts (Shuell, 1992). For example, an object could be rotated to be seen from various perspectives and objects can be presented so that the student can see the effect that different parameters have on the presented object or process. It is worth noting, however, that many static graphics can be shown on a page, so one should have a rationale for incorporating a significant number of static graphics in CBL. It is also suggested that designers should ensure that the graphics presented to the learner are relevant to the material to be learned (Shuell, 1992). Indeed, there are guidelines for the effective use of graphics in CBL materials (such as Clarke, 1992). Designers are advised, for example, to relate graphics to the capability you want to be learned and are told that 'a realistic picture may well gain the attention and interest of learners more easily than a basic drawing' (ibid., pp.71–3). Quite simply, the use of irrelevant presentations could distract the student from the learning task at hand (Shuell, 1992). With the aid of the computer, it is also possible to focus the learner on relevant features of a graphic or picture. This may be done through the use of techniques such as pop-ups or highlighting or, if appropriate, aspects of the graphical material could be magnified. Here, the issue of learner control is of importance: the learner for example, may want to have a more detailed representation for a specific part of a diagram, and at the click of a mouse the area of interest is magnified.

Second, computers can provide a variety of immediate feedback to the learner concerning their actions at the interface, or the adequacy of their responses (Shuell, 1992). This may be particularly useful if computer-based courseware makes use of self-assessment questions.

Third, if carefully designed, CBL can offer a learning environment in the form of a simulation programme or a microworld. In general, these can be set up to enable students to explore and investigate various options, and/or provide them with the opportunity to experiment with various actions and to see the consequences of such actions (Shuell, 1992). These three areas: visual dynamic displays, immediate feedback and simulation are to be exploited in the design of BioActive.

CBL DESIGN METHODS

For the design of BioActive, Laurillard's strategy for courseware development has been partly employed (Laurillard, 1993, pp.181–209). To design effective and appropriate learning materials it is suggested that:

(i)   the aims and objectives of the subject area are defined, and
(ii) students' learning needs are addressed and identified with reference to a checklist.

Shuell (1992) has formulated an approach to instructional design that is based on cognitive theories of meaningful learning and which advises the designer to

(i)   identify purpose and/or goals [of the instructional system]; and
(ii) consider the audience/user
      (Shuell, 1992, pp.45–6).

The audience or users of BioActive were considered and specified early on in the design process. Here, there is much overlap between these two CBL design methods, but the procedures to identify learning objectives and students' needs (Laurillard, 1993) were followed because if one is to compare (ii) in both of the above cases, a more thorough method is offered by Laurillard.

DEFINING LEARNING OBJECTIVES

The overall aims of the course 'Energy from biomass' are:

to examine the feasibility, both practically and economically, of using a variety of biological energy sources, all of which ultimately have been derived from light energy via the process of photosynthesis, as alternatives or additions to other sources of fuel currently used (Course Outline, 1993).

As part of this course, time is made available to introduce assignments which involve solutions or recommendations to real problems currently encountered (Course Outline). As a course requirement, students are to complete two such assignments which account for 20 per cent of the final mark for the course:

(a)   A proposal for an integrated energy system at Khandia, Gujarat.
(b)   Ethanol: Is it the fuel of the future? Guidelines for countries contemplating ethanol as a fuel.

BioActive is to support the work required for these two assignments and so those objectives from the original 14 learning objectives that had been outlined, which relate to the topic areas that should be covered and explored for the assignments, have been examined and revised partly with reference to the procedure outlined by Laurillard (1993). The assignments are assessed and marked in ways which outline points that should be considered in a student's report. These requirements have been included in the revised learning objectives, as shown in the examples below.

(a) Students' task: A proposal for an integrated energy system at Khandia, Gujarat

Relevant learning objectives
Students should be able to:

1. Present a well-organized and informative report.

2. State the advantages and possible problems of a proposed integrated energy system with reference to: the local people; the local government; the national government; and the environment.

3. Describe in outline the process and conditions necessary for maximizing the production of biogas in both small-scale and large-scale digesters.

4. List the main advantages and disadvantages of short rotation crop forestry and agrenforestry under the relevant climatic and environmental conditions. Recognize that particular species are suitable for an area or region.

5. Calculate and propose the capital cost of a proposed integrated energy system and the annual percentage return on investment.

6. Appropriately cite references that have been consulted.

(b) Students' task: Ethanol – is it the fuel of the future? Guidelines for countries contemplating ethanol as a fuel

Relevant learning objectives
Students should be able to:

1. Present a well-organized and informative report.

2. State the main sources of ethanol from biomass.

3. Outline ethanol production method(s).

4. Outline the process of alcoholic fermentation and the organisms and conditions affecting production of ethanol.

5. State and assess the benefits and costs of using ethanol as a fuel, taking into account economic, agricultural and environmental considerations. These should be made with reference to particular case studies:

       The Brazilian 'gasohol' programme.
       The US 'gasohol' programme.
       The Zimbabwe ethanol programme.

6.   Indicate the main areas of research aimed at improving ethanol production (including valuable byproducts) with minimum pollution.

7.   Describe the advantages and disadvantages of using fuel ethanol.

8.   Provide a summary of recommendations in using fuel ethanol.

9.   Appropriately cite references that have been consulted.

IDENTIFYING STUDENTS' NEEDS

To address and identify students' needs, students' assignments have been examined in the light of the above requirements and the following possible pitfalls have been considered:

● What technical terms have everyday meanings that could lead to their misinterpretation?

● What kinds of naive conceptions might be prevalent in this topic [subject area]?

● What forms of representation (linguistic, ...diagrammatic, graphical, symbolic... numeric) are difficult to handle? (Laurillard, 1993, p.193).

With the first assignment on an integrated energy system at Khandia, a number of students encountered and presented the following problems:

● Failure to present a well-organized report. For example, material is not sectioned.

● Failure to appropriately cite references and/or consult references. (In addition, titles or sources of tables for data and/or flow diagrams are not presented.)

● The calculation and proposal of the capital cost of the proposed system and the annual percentage return on investment is not included.

● Inaccurate calculations of the cost of the system and percentage return on investment.

● No (or very little) reference or comparisons are made to other relevant energy schemes.

In addition, the following were apparent:

- The rate of a biomass yield is described in terms of tonnes per hectare, where it should be tonnes per hectare per year (or another unit of time).

- To suggest the use of human waste for a biogas plant in rural areas of India is in fact inappropriate (see Rajabapaiah *et al.*, 1993).

In the second example, problems included:

- Failure to present other sources of ethanol from biomass aside from sugar cane and maize.

- A lack of detail given in ethanol production methods. For example, wet and dry milling are not described.

- The point of view of an agricultural economist is not covered sufficiently.

- Failure to consult and/or appropriately cite references (if at all).

- Failure to indicate the main areas of research aimed at improving ethanol production (including valuable byproducts), for example, the use of 'new' yeast strains/micro-organisms.

- Failure to present a well-organized report.

- The creation of employment opportunities within a region/country is not mentioned as an advantage in considering fuel ethanol production. This is evident from the Brazilian 'gasohol' programme (see Goldemberg *et al.*, 1993).

- Failure to consider that although job opportunities may be created by the biomass industry, this does not ensure a good standard of job quality. (For example, the Brazilian sugar cane workers provide cheap labour for ethanol production [see Goldemberg *et al.*, 1993]).

In addition, it was apparent that:

- The relative suitability and availability of land for biomass (plantations of energy crops) were not addressed with respect to how this may differ between countries. For example, the success of the Brazilian programme is taken to indicate that EU countries could adopt a similar scheme. This is made with no discussion of the land that is, or is not, available for energy crops in rather smaller countries (see Hall *et al.*, 1993).

- Students failed to outline the possible use of degraded land for biomass plantations in developing countries and the positive implications of this.

- Students failed to outline the use of excess cropland for biomass in industrialized countries (see Hall *et al.*, 1993).

- Students showed a tendency to use the Brazilian and USA ethanol programmes as examples, rather than others such as Zimbabwe (see Scurloch *et al.*, 1991).

DESIGNING THE LEARNING MATERIALS AND ACTIVITIES

It has been decided that BioActive is to provide multimedia and learning activities or tasks. Having outlined the learning objectives and/or the requirements of the two assignments and highlighted those areas where students typically encounter and present problems, it is now necessary to use this information to guide the design of the application. This information could be used to answer the questions: 'What material, in the form of text and graphics for example, should be provided?' 'What learning activities and tasks should be provided?' In this respect, subject topics that were to be covered or included in BioActive were identified and organized. In addition, material in the form of graphics and diagrams were specified and suggestions of learning activities to supplement various topics were documented. For example, it is proposed that the topic '4.3 The design of biogas plants' will present not only photographic images of different biogas plant designs, but:

> a dynamic interactive graphic: to show gas production – where gas production depends on the amount and type of dung, the ambient temperature, and pH (parameters that the student can vary and will show the consequences, eg a decrease in gas production) (The Design of the Learning Materials and Activities, p.6).

This approach, however, does not necessarily ensure that the resulting CBL system will be educationally valid. Shuell (1992) argues that if CBL systems are to be instructionally or educationally valid then they must be based on a thorough understanding of how students learn from instruction. He also suggests that in order for a student to learn from instruction various psychological processes must occur in the learner. Specifically, he proposes 12 learning functions which must be 'engaged by either the instructional agent or the student if effective learning is to occur and that each function can be elicited in a number of equally effective ways' (ibid., p.19).

More importantly, a prescriptive and principled approach is provided for the design of CBL: the learning functions can be incorporated into a system indirectly by, for example, designing the interface or the program in ways that increase the likelihood that particular or various learning functions are engaged. For example, the learning function 'prior knowledge activation' should occur if meaningful learning is to take place, and it can either be initiated by the teacher/system through the use of various techniques such as reminding the learner of relevant and appropriate information that they have recently learned or the function can be student initiated where, for example, the student is prompted to ask themselves what is already known about the topic in question (see Shuell, 1992, Table 1, p.31). This is the nitty-gritty of this instructional approach, but the instruction design process that is proposed directs the designer to acknowledge and incorporate the learning functions by means of the following method:

- specify instructional procedures
- present the knowledge that is to be acquired
- motivate the learner
- engage those psychological processes [learning functions] necessary for learning to occur (Shuell, 1992, p.45).

Having identified the purpose and/or goals of BioActive by defining learning objectives and anticipated the users of the system (both in general terms and in terms of their [possible] learning needs), this method is to be followed for the variety of subject topics that will be presented in BioActive. These subject topics that are to be included were identified and organized with reference to the defined learning objectives and the identified students' learning needs as described above.

A sample topic

Topic 8. Why biomass conversion to fuel ethanol has been identified as useful for the completion of the assignment in which students must complete a set of guidelines for countries considering fuel ethanol. The *instructional procedures* include three interrelated factors that were considered for this topic:

- present the knowledge that is to be acquired;
- motivate the learner;
- engage those psychological processes [learning functions] necessary for learning to occur.

Accordingly, the *knowledge* that the student should acquire is the main reason for using biomass to provide liquid motor fuels:

- Environmental reasons: there is the need to remove toxic lead from petrol (gasoline), and to use ethanol in its place. Gasoline is a major source of urban smog, while the use of fuel ethanol improves air quality.
- There is a need to make use of surplus crops, which are a major problem in Europe and North America.
- Biomass is a renewable resource that could provide motor fuels in the long term, whereas the sources of petroleum will eventually run out.

However, before such knowledge is presented to the learner, the system should *motivate* him or her. This is done by reminding the student of the assignment that they are to complete and by directing them to environmental issues that may provide an interest and a reason to find out more about the uses of fuel ethanol. This topic is also (hopefully) enhanced by the use of a photographic image that is to be presented on screen.

It is also advised that the system (or the learner) *engage those psychological processes* necessary for meaningful learning. For instance, before the knowledge is presented, the student is asked:

● Can you think of some reasons why biomass should be used to provide liquid motor fuels? (prior knowledge activation).

Having presented the three main reasons to the learner, the following questions and task are presented at the interface:

● But is the production and use of biofuels from biomass free from technical, economic and environmental problems?

● Think of a particular country of your choice and let's say it is considering a large-scale fuel ethanol programme.

  – Why should this country use fuel ethanol?
  – What are the major problems this country faces in the production and use of fuel ethanol? (hypothesis generation).

SUPPORTING PAIRS

Computers are often seen as learning tools that can potentially enhance cooperative learning (O'Malley, 1992). In addition, it has been suggested that a type of peer-teaching method known as 'learning cells' or 'dyads' where students read and/or discuss in pairs is beneficial, encourages students to take responsibility for their learning and leads to more of an involvement in the learning process (Entwistle *et al.*, 1992). To encourage discussion and to facilitate learning, BioActive is designed to be used by students working in pairs. There has, however, been little progress in looking at how one might design CBL specifically for students working together (O'Malley, 1992).

As a straightforward approach to support students, BioActive will present questions to suggest discussion between students for the subject topics that have been organized. The application of Shuell's (1992) instructional method to subject topics can provide questions to motivate and direct the learner. These questions can be used as discussion points to support students working as pairs.

CONTEXT

It is recognized that the success of new learning materials depends primarily on the way that they are integrated into courses (Laurillard, 1993). Designers and developers must anticipate the learning context in which the new technology will be used. Computer-based courseware should not be developed in isolation, separate from the course it is meant to enhance or support. Rather, the design must explicitly address the areas of a course it is to replace or supplement. It is fortunate, therefore, that the development of BioActive was initiated and is fully supported by the organizer and lecturer of the course, 'Energy from biomass' (M Tribe). Moreover, as has been noted previously, the system has a fairly specific role to play on an existing course: to support the research and study necessary for the two assignments that are a requirement of the course.

Research studies of the implementation of programmes in classrooms show that they are most successful when students are properly prepared and know what to expect when they use the programme (Laurillard, 1993). Accordingly, it is suggested that developers should provide a teacher guide (and/or student guides) to the use of the learning materials. This is to ensure that the materials are integrated into the course, used appropriately, and that the students make optimum use of the systems facilities. If students are to make effective and efficient use of computer-based courseware, then this activity should be directed by a particular study task. A student guide can prepare them so they make appropriate use of a systems resources. The evaluation of the first prototype of BioActive with students in the spring of 1995 will determine whether such a guide or preparation worksheet is necessary.

CONCLUSIONS

This chapter has addressed a number of issues that arise in the design of CBL. User-centred design is essential for the successful development of computer-based courseware: prototypes must be modified and improved in response to students' evaluations. Quality developmental testing and evaluation, however, does take significant time, effort and expertise. Moreover, there are many evaluation methods and techniques that focus on the usability of software (e.g. Monk *et al.*, 1993), but there is a lack of literature concerning the evaluation of CBL: educational technology must be more that just pleasant and easy to learn and use. System development must begin with a requirements specification. The completion of this is an essential and valuable exercise which serves to focus ideas, specify delivery requirements, and identify functions. To ensure that CBL materials and products are, in fact, used, the design process must also seriously consider a variety of factors so that appropriate design decisions can be made. The courseware developers must, for example, consider the particular needs of a course and the students, and the wider learning context in which the learning materials will be incorporated.

Methods for computer-based courseware do exist (Laurillard, 1993; Shuell, 1992) and the employment of such design methods may lead to CBL materials that can be described as educationally valid. Yet there are aspects of Laurillard's (1993) strategy for courseware design that are not necessarily easy to follow and the approach to instructional design (Shuell, 1992) can also at times be confusing and difficult to adopt. For example, Shuell (1992) lists 12 learning functions or psychological processes that should be engaged by the system or by the learner. He also suggests a number of ways or techniques that can be employed to ensure that such processes occur. It is not clear whether each of the 12 functions and their associated techniques should be applied for each individual topic identified for the subject area and/or for a general learning objective. To illustrate: the function expectations, where the learner should have an clear idea of what he or she is trying to accomplish, can be achieved by providing a graphical overview of the programme or a set of learning objectives, a technique that would affect the learning of many topics that are covered by the programme. Accordingly, when the designer applies particular methods or techniques (that are associated with particular learning functions) to a topic area, some of the learning functions are not of direct concern or relevance. In other words, Shuell (1992) does not make explicit the level that the techniques should be applied. More importantly, however, is the fact that these methods are time-consuming, and although we doubt that they require specific expertise, they certainly require much thought and consideration. Accordingly, their full use in the design of CBL may be inappropriate and unrealistic.

The approach described in this chapter could be used in other situations where student cooperation in decision making is desirable. There are certainly many current issues where science, technology, economics and society converge and where computer-based courseware could be valuable. For example, issues (both ethical and technical) relating to inherited disorders such as Huntington's disease, thalassaemia and cystic fibrosis; medical issues such as AIDS, organ transplants, *in vitro* fertilization, the prolongation of life, to cite just a few. Above all, it is important that students are provided with opportunities to work together and apply their knowledge in real-world situations. CBL should be seen as an integral part of a total learning package, incorporating library facilities, lectures, practicals and all other aspects of learning that students will encounter.

REFERENCES

Clarke, A (1992) *The Principles of Screen Design for Computer Based Learning Materials. Learning methods project report*, Employment Department, Sheffield.

Cox, K and Walker, D (1993) *User Interface Design*, Prentice-Hall, New York.

Dix, A J, Finlay, J, Abowd, G and Beale, R (1993) *Human Computer Interaction*, Prentice-Hall, New York.

Entwistle, N (1991) *The Impact of Teaching on Learning Outcomes in Higher Education. Review of the literature for the Enterprise in Higher Education Initiative*, Department of Employment, Sheffield.

Entwistle, N, Thompson, S, and Tait, H (1992) *Guidelines for Promoting Effective Learning in Higher Education*, Centre for Research on Learning and Instruction, Edinburgh.

Goldemberg, J, Monaco, L C, and Macedo, I C (1993) 'The Brazilian fuel-alcohol program', in Johansson, T B *et al.* (eds) *Renewable Energy: Sources for Fuels and Electricity*, Island Press, Washington DC.

Hall, D O, Rosillo-Calle, F, Williams, R H and Woods, J (1993) 'Biomass for energy: supply prospects', in Johansson *et al.* (eds), *Renewable Energy* (op. cit.).

Hammond, N (1993) 'Learning with Hypertext: problems, principles and prospects', in McKnight, C, Dillon, A and Richardson, J (eds) *Hypertext: A Psychological Perspective*, Ellis Horwood, New York.

Laurillard, D (1993) *Rethinking University Teaching: A Framework for the Effective Use of Educational Technology*, Routledge, London.

Marsh, E J and Kumar, D D (1992) 'Hypermedia: A conceptual framework for science education and review of recent findings', *Journal of Educational Multimedia and Hypermedia*, 1, 25–37.

Monk, A, Wright, P, Haber, J and Davenport, L (1993) *Improving Your Human-Computer Interface: a Practical Technique*, Prentice Hall, New York.

O'Malley, C (1992) 'Designing computer systems to support peer learning', *European Journal of Psychology of Education*, VII, 4, 339–52.

Preece, J (ed) (1993) *A Guide to Usability: Human factors in computing*, Addison-Wesley, Wokingham.

Rajabapaiah, P, Jayakumar, S and Reddy, A K N (1993) 'Biogas electricity – the Pura Village case study', in Johansson *et al.* (eds), *Renewable Energy* (op. cit.).

Scurlock, J, Rosenschein, A and Hall, D O (1991) *Fuelling the Future. Power alcohol in Zimbabwe*, Acts Press, African Centre for Technology Studies, Nairobi, Kenya.

Shuell, T J (1992) 'Designing instructional computing systems for meaningful learning', in Jones, M and Winne, P H (eds), *Adaptive Learning Environments*, Springer-Verlag, Berlin.

Chapter 13

Establishing Enabling Practices in Postgraduate Student Supervision

Gina Wisker

INTRODUCTION

More of us in HE are taking on the supervision of research students, particularly if we work, as I do, in a new university which seeks to develop its research culture alongside its teaching culture. What has struck me in my triple role as ex-research student, supervisor and staff developer, is that there is an enormous diversity of practices in supervising postgraduate or research students, with little sharing of guidelines and successful practices, and there is a great deal we could all learn from much of our work with undergraduates and our own work as researchers.

The research student is expected to work relatively autonomously on a project or area of research which is to some extent their own and original. They are also meant to work with, and to, a research supervisor who will to some extent share their interests and area of expertise, and who probably has many other tasks to carry out associated with being an academic member of the teaching staff in a UK university, that is, administrative, teaching and management tasks and their own research. Frequently the supervisor is unsure exactly in what ways they can usefully work with and guide the research student, often because of that autonomy, and their other tasks. In many universities they are often also working in the context of guidelines which are either broad and bland, or non-existent. One thing we might feel when starting to supervise students is that we are ourselves rather left out in the open, drifting, unsure of the regulations and how to interpret them, unsure of how much we can help students without over-interfering, how much we are supposed to do to support them and what other support or enabling systems and practices are in place elsewhere.

In many ways, supervision can be one of the most rewarding teaching and learning experiences all round. Our supervision sessions with our research students are a marvellous opportunity for both of us to discuss our specialist areas and share discoveries and questions.

In order to better enable our research students to carry out their research successfully, we need to look closely at expectations, problems, systems and good practices of supervision, and consider further how we can work with our students, within the university system, helping them to help themselves. In short we need to consider how best to provide the necessary supervision and support, and to provide also the enabling practices which will help students to get on with and successfully complete the research themselves.

CONTEXT AT ANGLIA: EXPERIENCES, SYSTEMS, PRACTICES AND STAFF DEVELOPMENT ISSUES

Recently I have run a number of staff development workshop sessions which seek to address different groups and different concerns and practices of supervising research students. One strand of the development sessions is for research students, while another focuses on staff supervising or about to supervise research students, often for the first time. Unless they are very new to teaching, staff have all had experience in the supervision of undergraduate research projects and dissertations.

It is from the interesting interface between these sessions that this chapter has developed. Both halves of the supervisor/supervised equation seek to find ways in which they can work well together, giving and receiving support which does not paralyse and contain but instead enables development, thought, work, originality and the production of a research thesis.

What has been brought home to me is the importance of developing for research students some of the best practices related to the encouragement of student autonomy, group work and peer support which are currently working well in many undergraduate degree programmes. It is with these, and guidelines for best practice in general, in mind that we have explored together in both sets of staff development sessions:

- stages of setting up, defining and organizing the research supervision area and the research supervision process;
- issues about the 'special relationship' between supervisor and research student which need managing;
- guidelines, good experiences, good practices of supervising students and of enabling them to carry out their own research work;
- suggestions on where the supervisor fits into the equation of support, supervision, autonomy;
- issues of managing the project, time, the research students and the supervisor – from all perspectives;
- ideas about supervising research students at a distance;
- thoughts about supervising research students full- and part-time;

- issues associated with supervising colleagues who are also your research students.

Developing good practice takes place in the context of our understanding of the kinds of problems which might occur with postgraduate students and their studies. Some points which have emerged from staff development sessions and materials of use to supervisors, new or established, focus on staff needs and on students' concerns and needs.

Although there are often guidelines about submission dates, length, even hours of supervisory work, there are few about the actual conduct of the supervisor's role. It is useful to look at this, considering the stages of the students' research, the role and practice of the supervisor, and the kinds of structures and systems which staff and students can set up to enable well supervised quality research to take place.

Staff need clarification about:

- amount of supervision or direction;

- selection of topic or research project;

- frequency and content of meetings;

- approaches to supervision;

- personal relations with students;

- dealing with postgraduate students' problems.

KEY ISSUES AND SUGGESTIONS

We advise that:

- the supervisor should ensure that the student is engaged on a promising topic which should produce sufficient results within time limits;

- the supervisor should assist students to develop standards of achievement that will result in a thesis of merit (adapted from University of Queensland Calendar, CAPA, 1985).

Issues of how to supervise in an enabling way feed into the production of guidelines reflecting the work we can carry out as supervisors, stages in the development of the research project and specific support and enabling systems which could encourage and empower students to run their own research and manage their own learning. Broadly, some issues are:

- ensuring clarity of roles and responsibilities;

- encouraging informed responsible autonomy;

- using learning contracts;
- supervising group/project team;
- organising group/project team self-managed sessions;
- establishing networks and peer group support systems.

The context of the student's research work

For the research student of today there is often a need to earn money, so rare are full-time grants for research. Many students at Anglia and elsewhere study on a contract relating them to a research unit which sometimes actually lasts for only two years, while their PhD will last for at least three. For students working in a team alongside staff employed on a project by the university, it is very important to balance the time spent on the research with other duties the university might request, such as teaching and assessment or other departmental activities. It is also important that their research is aligned with university projects. Those involved in part-time study and funded elsewhere by their own work have a little more opportunity to develop their own ideas and slant their research in relation to findings and personal choice, all within the general outline of the research proposal. Still others are working, perhaps, abroad, as one of my students is, and in these cases there are so many more variables, not merely of communication but perhaps of cultural difference, as well as potential difficulties in achieving the research aims in different contexts and perhaps more volatile situations.

It is helpful to look closely at the stages of development of a research student's project from proposal through to writing up so that the postgraduate supervisor can see in what ways and at what points they can enable the student's development.

STAGES OF POSTGRADUATE RESEARCH: THE SUPERVISOR'S INVOLVEMENT AND GOOD PRACTICE

Some potential students approach us because they know we work in areas in which they are interested, while others are directed to us by the central research office and still others respond to advertisements for researchers on projects. Once the supervisor has been recognized and contacts made, there follow informal interviews or discussions, perhaps by phone or letter. The early development of an outline of the student's hypothesis, ideas, concerns and research questions follow, along with initial ideas on the literature which they would consult in their research. It is at this stage that the supervisor helps the student to formulate a viable project (or not), based on the quality of the research questions, the methodology, the student's ability to organize the ideas and their discoveries to date, and to change and develop ideas in relation to what they are discovering.

Supervisors need to follow internal regulations. In many of the new universities, it is common for there to be a director of studies and a second internal supervisor plus an external supervisor. The first supervisor or the student him/herself might be in a position to suggest the other two. It is a good idea to pick someone who is interested in the same ideas and area but perhaps can contribute different skills, such as methodology skills and different contacts. The external supervisor is also useful for their relative objectivity and other contacts and angles on the research.

The supervisor needs to ensure that the student draws up a credible and viable research outline and discussion of whatever length is required by the internal processes. They also need to discuss the methodology with the student and to ascertain the kinds of research questions and outcomes expected, kinds of probable skills, data gathering and processing, in ideology, in theory, and so on which the student foresees.

The student and supervisor need to be in agreement about the proposal which goes before the research degrees committees as it will be thoroughly read, probably by both an internal and an external referee who will have points to make about the viability, the expression and the methodology. It is tempting if the research proposal is accepted just to ignore the questions asked at a research degrees committee, but in fact some questions about contexts, methods and so on are very helpful in the formation of arguments and in the discovery of information and ideas.

The supervisor and students need to set up a regular system of supervision so that the student feels that they can have a formal exchange about the development of their project when they need it, that is, when they meet difficulties or have developed a reasonable amount of work. The supervisor will not want to be contacted excessively (or they will worry about unduly influencing the work), and the research student might well feel awkward about regular contacts because they are unsure of how much the supervisor can be involved. It has been noted by Moses (1985) that often there are too many merely informal contacts. The supervisor and student who see each other regularly are less likely to concentrate in informal discussions on the specific research questions and discoveries of the student, and more in social discussions. It is important for the student that they maintain this sociable conversation but that they do not let all their supervisions degenerate into chats walking along a corridor, or generalized discussions over a cup of tea. It is imperative to develop a system of a somewhat more formal supervision with agendas on both sides, so that the precious time can be used for the most part in addressing the research questions, problems and needs of the student and in giving feedback, once work has been completed, on what has been achieved so as to enable the student to progress.

This is a long-term relationship. It is important that all parties are very clear about their roles and responsibilities and ensure that they feel they can work together, even if they are not necessarily friends.

One of the central concerns of various pieces written about research supervision concentrates on difficulties of personality clash and indeed, some research students never write up or complete because of such problems. It is important that both halves of this relationship recognise the limitations, expectations and responsibilities of the relationship so that undue strain is not placed upon it, and so that the student also knows when, where and on what issues they might contact their supervisor, so that too much or too little contact are avoided. Clarifying the key stages of research work to be undertaken and written up, and ensuring that students are aware of roles, responsibilities, rights, rules and regulations can all aid the development of smooth working relationships, and help develop relatively autonomous students enabled in their work and successful in research.

Planning the research is an important first stage and supervisors need to encourage students to:

- state the research problem, looking at the introduction, the nature of the problem, why it is important and how research will contribute to its solution;

- state the research question or hypothesis, in the form of an interrogative statement asking the relationship between variables, phenomena and events, including definitions of terms;

- decide on subsidiary questions;

- carry out a review of relevant research and theory: not a disjointed summary, but an integrated statement which affords insights into why theories and so on are important to the proposed work.

The next stage is to move towards establishing the procedure which, particularly in a science research project, should contain a description of the theoretical or conceptual framework, a list of potential reading and other sources of evidence and authority, an outline of the analytical techniques, the methodologies to be used, and of the research design. There should also be a timetable for the completion of stages of the work, and a draft set of contents which helps the student to define the major areas of work and research questions informing the whole.

Some of the stages and some of the responsibilities include network planning or critical path analysis and involve setting objectives, ordering research activities, estimating the time each stage of the research should take, deciding on and ordering or getting hold of the necessary facilities and resources, and drawing up a realistic schedule which will, of course, be changed with developments, setbacks and changes in circumstances. Some of these stages and our responsibilities as supervisors can be summarized as follows:

- establishing a research role model;

- teaching the strategies of research;

- ensuring students carry out any necessary preliminary other skill development and study, for example, research methods, statistics training;

- helping students shape initial plans;
- helping students refine and define the field, methodology, scope and nature of the research;
- encouraging realistic approaches and hopes;
- putting contacts and reading material their way;
- encouraging early outlines and the refining of these outlines;
- encouraging the development of good time-management habits;
- setting up a pattern of supervision early on, which can be modified as necessary;
- putting students in touch with other research students;
- helping to design useful learning situations and taking advantage of openings which could help students develop;
- staying in touch but not intruding unless necessary;
- caring;
- reading students' work thoroughly;
- considering students' questions, and the questions they should be asking;
- helping to tease out difficult issues and problems;
- giving constructive criticism;
- weaning students into autonomy, gently and gradually;
- encouraging academic role development;
- encouraging students to start to write up as soon as they can, and to alter their work if necessary (but not leaving it too late);
- looking at early drafts of work;
- encouraging editing, helping them to shape and rewrite if necessary;
- encouraging students to take part in academic activities such as conferences, to gain information, share ideas and try out ideas on others;
- selecting a suitable external examiner;
- briefing and supporting the student prior to examination;
- encouraging further work and publishing of findings.

Being aware of these stages and taking notice of the advice can help supervisor and student develop a harmonious working relationship with clear patterns and expectations of responsibilities. However, there are some specific areas in which students can have problems in their research, or with their supervisor.

Students have problems with:

- *personality factors*:

    neglect by supervisor,
    clash of personalities,
    barriers to communication arising from age, class, gender, race,
    differences in approach to work.

- *professional factors:*

    misinformed supervisor, or supervisor without sufficient knowledge in
    the area supervised,
    supervisor with few genuine research interests, or ones which differ
    fundamentally from those of the student.

- *organizational factors:*

    supervisor having too many students to supervise,
    supervisor too busy with administrative work,
    supervisor unable to manage their research group or their numbers of
    researchers efficiently,
    isolation of students in departments and faculties due to inadequate
    arrangements,
    inadequate support services and provision of equipment.
    (Phillips and Pugh, 1992).

Some of these problems can be avoided if the supervisor ensures they take on only as many students as they can reasonably work with, all of whom are working in areas with which they have some expertise and interest. It is important to ensure, as far as possible, that appropriate resources and equipment are made available, and that students are put in touch with the university's and wider community's research culture and its activities, so they can start forming supportive working relationships with other research students, whether in their own field or not. This starts to wean them away from dependency and helps them to develop autonomy in their work, without the supervisor neglecting the student's needs. Enabling students to find support among their peers and central resources, as well as ensuring that we all act professionally, go a long way to aiding the student's autonomy in research and to overcoming any awkward relations.

Research also suggests that student dissatisfaction can be avoided if there is clear and open communication on all aspects of the project and an overall structure without a straitjacket, which facilitates rather than hinders students' development and creativity. Such a structure will enable students to develop their autonomy, sure of the rules and resources, and sure of the intellectual and systematic support they need to do so. It will also help students to each get a similar fair deal when being supervised, even in cases where they have personality clashes with supervisors.

Students can expect their supervisors to:

- *supervise:* guide as to structure, scope, decisions about methodology and so on, indicating if the research goes off beam;

- *read their work thoroughly,* and in advance, mentioning areas which need curtailing and shaping;

- *be available when needed:* they need to be planning regular supervisions, but also be able to make visits to ask key questions, through a 'surgery' or other system;

- *be friendly, open and supportive:* academic issues need discussion but it is important to establish a consultative, supportive relationship too;

- *be constructively critical:* praise should be given where relevant, criticism toned to the constructive rather than the harsh, to enable productive change. If they do not receive helpful information and feedback they might become discouraged. Gradually they will need less support as autonomy and judgement develop;

- *have a good knowledge of the research area.* If you are not an expert, provided the student has access to others who are, you can still supervise and support;

- *structure the supervisions,* and ongoing relationship so that it is relatively easy to exchange ideas;

- *have sufficient interest in their research* to put more information their way;

- *be sufficiently involved* in their success to help them get a good job at the end of it all.
  (Adapted from Phillips and Pugh, 1992).

In order to best enable the learning of their students, supervisors need to learn how to ask open questions, how to draw out ideas and problems and how to elicit information even if the student finds communication difficult. Some of this can be facilitated by working for some of the time with more than one student present, to aid discussion.

There is often a concern about how much supervisors are actually involved in the work the students carry out. We are important in helping to shape and structure the work, and in providing support, information and guidance, but we must not actually do the work for the students ourselves. When the drafts of the thesis finally come in, it is important that the supervisor is involved in encouraging some of the editing but not actually carrying it out themselves. Discussing fundamental theories and the meaning of what has been discovered is helpful, but final expression and editing is not. It starts to take the ownership of the work away from the student. The supervisor should be the repository of knowledge about rules and regulations concerning expression, layout and so on but it is important that the student has the written information about these details and access to central information, as we as supervisors sometimes forget and give false or scanty information. With information and formalized rules and systems of support established, understood and available, the student is empowered and responsible to make choices, develop and express ideas and finally to check that expression themselves in their final draft of the thesis.

To avoid problems, supervisors have to negotiate with students at the outset where different responsibilities lie and to agree with them what roles and responsibilities they will each take on. It is in the spirit of this need that the idea of contracts emerges while an ongoing need for support and discussion produces peer support systems and co-counselling. Difficulties of research students working at a distance provoke development of distance systems and a different kind of pacing of agreed activities. Some of these needs can be satisfied by the development of contracts, and some others by peer support networks and structures.

Contracts

It is important for the sake of clarity and equality that learning contracts clearly define how much time is available, what kind of support supervisors can offer, and what the expected behaviours of both students and supervisors are. Learning contracts can be drawn up which make expectations explicit, such as frequency of supervisions and the production of stages of work. These can help both halves of the supervisory equation to manage their work (Wisker and Sutcliffe, forthcoming).

Group/project team supervisions

In some subject areas such as practical science or medicine, there are likely to be several students working on a related project. In these cases, it would be useful to hold regular group project supervisions at which students can share ideas, problems and questions, and supervisors can say once some of the things that would otherwise be repeated individually, about learning outcomes, length of the thesis, time, protocols, question framing, strategies, reading and so on. In other subject areas there might be only one student working in a specific area, but there will probably be a few working in cognate areas or areas which are otherwise related, whether in terms of methodology being used, or in terms of subject or discipline. It would be useful in these instances to bring these students together regularly or occasionally for group supervisions. This is not to substitute for individual supervisions, but to augment these and provide a sense of sharing, support and peer responsibility. They will get as much out of sharing their own questions and ideas and work in progress with each other as in discussing it with supervisors, and group sessions will enable them to keep supervisors updated on their progress, and give them the opportunity to ask questions and to seek to develop ideas.

Self-managed groups and networks

The sharing of key questions about procedures, systems and ideas, depending on the context, can be immensely useful for students who might otherwise feel rather isolated. Not only does a group help students to feel supported and to discuss issues, developments, problems and breakthroughs, but it can also provide the perfect opportunity for that very exploratory talk which we all value so much at undergraduate level, but which seems often sorely missing just when it is absolutely essential to the development of enquiry, the testing of hypotheses and the sharing of discoveries, at postgraduate level. One role as supervisor might be to put research students who work with you, or who work with your colleagues, in touch with each other, suggesting they form self-managed groups and supportive networks.

Such groups can meet regularly to discuss questions in each others' research, share skills in literature searches, pilot questionnaires and so on, and hear reports on each others' work in progress, providing useful feedback and sharing ideas.

Networks can aid the dissemination of skills and information and keep students in touch with each other. With this kind of communication, not only can they support each other and discuss ideas and findings and so on, but also they can keep each other in touch on issues of dates, regulations, passing the hurdle of transfer to PhD from MPhil and other such potentially threatening, often confused and ill-informed experiences.

It is probable that the supervisor will play a key role in setting up these self-managed groups and networks to begin with, but they should then be able to run on their own, driven by the students, because they are useful to them.

General staff and student development sessions

It has been found (Gibbs *et al.*, 1995) to be particularly helpful to both supervisors and students that there should be facilitated sessions to look at the developments in the role, stresses, demands and success stories in terms of guidelines and practices. Out of such sessions have come some shared agreement and clarity of practices, awareness of problems and needs, sharing of concerns and solutions over time management, managing the stage of the project, finding and using facilities and getting along with each other.

Some of the issues on which I have worked with the researchers and students have related closely to those concentrated on in the sessions with supervisors. Such guidelines thus produced are a direct match to those for supervisors, and might be of use in checking through with research students in the initial stages of their work, so that they can see where their roles and responsibilities lie and where lie those of their supervisors, so that they can consider the other forms of support they need, how to make the best of enabling structures, and how to make the best of their own resources.

Other peer support systems: establishing a research culture

A key peer support system and a very good one for developing the skill of research, is the research seminar series. During this both staff and students give research-in-progress seminar papers followed by discussions. Here questions can be asked and methodology, practices, discoveries, theories and problems all aired and discussed, with a coherent base of a seminar paper upon which to build.

CONCLUSION

These examples contribute to the development of practices and culture which clarify the supervisor's role, releasing them from the kind of hand-holding childminding role which over-dependence can produce. Similarly it prevents chaos, where the research student does not know who to turn to and is unsure whether they can ask questions of their possibly quite elusive supervisor (who is probably flat out, giving lectures and marking on another part of the campus, involved in the myriad of areas of work of a contemporary academic's life).

Autonomy, negotiation and the development of shared responsibilities should result from these practices, placing supervisors as facilitators and ensuring students are well-informed of formats, rules, dates, demands, sure of what to expect of supervision, and with peer groups helping them share ideas and develop a sense both of communicative peer support and ownership of their work. Contracts clarify expectations, responsibilities and relationships, while as useful additions to formal, timetabled supervision sessions peer and group-based sessions and systems can make life easier and much more productive all round. A lower dropout rate and better quality of work are predictable, tangible results.

REFERENCES

Council of Australian Postgraduate Associations (1985) *University of Queensland Calendar,* Brisbane, University of Queensland Press.
Gibbs, G, Wisker, G and Bochner, D (1995) *Supporting More Students,* Oxford, Oxford Centre for Staff Development.
Moses, I (1985) *Supervising Postgraduates,* HERDSA Green Guides No. 3, Sydney, HERDSA.
Phillips, E and Pugh, D S (1992) *How to Get a PhD,* Open University Press, Buckingham.
Wisker, G and Sutcliffe, N (eds) (forthcoming) *Postgraduate Research Supervision,* SEDA, Birmingham.

Chapter 14

Support for New Supervisors of Research Students

Stephen J Fallows

INTRODUCTION

University academic staff are traditionally recruited on the basis of their research track record rather than their ability as teachers or lecturers. The skills needed to develop and deliver a coordinated, taught, course of study for students at both undergraduate and postgraduate levels are increasingly topics of staff development for the novice lecturer. Many institutions now offer a range of support from timetabled courses leading to formal qualifications to programmes of self-study and mentor support. The paradox of recruiting researchers to be lecturers is just one aspect of a potential HE skills gap which requires support for the novice. A second and, at least for the students concerned, potentially more damaging situation arises when universities take the view that the possession of a personal research track record automatically enables an academic staff member to supervise the work of students aiming for MPhil or PhD research degrees.

This chapter seeks to place this concern into its current context and to examine a number of the strategies which are undertaken to provide support for the novice supervisor. Key examples are taken from my own work at the University of Luton, an institution which was required to demonstrate its support systems and procedures to a panel convened by the HEQC as part of its successful bid for research degree-awarding powers. Here I contrast the very supportive systems which were needed to gain these powers with the less defined and often ad hoc procedures which apply in a number of older universities which have held the power to award research degrees for many years.

CONTEXT

The quality of supervision given by university staff to their research students undertaking MPhil or PhD degrees has become an increasingly significant issue in recent years. It is an issue of concern to those organizations which fund research studentships, to the universities and not least to the students and their supervisors. The funding organizations have become much more critical in their examination of applications for support and are looking closely at institutional prior performance (usually measured by thesis submission rates) when making decisions concerning new or continued funding. A number of institutions for which submission rates have been (to say the least) mediocre have been removed from the lists of those deemed suitable for support.

It follows inevitably from the above that the senior staff of those institutions which are deemed not to be suitable for funding will express their concern and will look for improvement in order that the institution's status may be raised.

Meanwhile, the changing national employment patterns are increasingly demanding success from both student and supervisor. The student will wish to be able to demonstrate successful degree completion to a potential employer (whether or not the intended employment requires the achievement of this degree) while the supervisor's performance will often include judgement on his or her students' successes.

This pressure for quality and success comes at a time when an increasing number of institutions have powers to award research degrees and many more members of academic staff are being encouraged to undertake research degree supervision. This inevitably raises the level of concern still further.

EXPERIENCE FROM ENGLAND'S NEWEST UNIVERSITY

It was against the context of the above concerns that the systems now in place at the University of Luton were established in a conscious effort to ensure that the quality of the research student experience was maximized within the inevitable constraints faced by an institution with relatively little prior experience of research degree supervision.

The University of Luton was until July 1993 the Luton College of Higher Education and during the 1970s and 1980s had only a very small number of students registered for research degrees through CNAA. By the beginning of the 1990s change was very apparent. The College aimed to become recognized as a polytechnic by 1992 but achieved all the required criteria just as the government announced its intention to create no more polytechnics and removed the binary divide. In order to progress further, (for designation as a university) the then college had to demonstrate to the HEQC, acting on behalf of the Privy Council, that its research degree procedures were robust enough to ensure (amongst other matters) that supervision would be of the best quality possible. In April 1993 the College's procedures were scrutinized closely by an HEQC panel and, following a positive recommendation by this panel, the College was granted university status in July 1993 as the first institution to be so designated under the aegis of the HEQC criteria and procedures.

The systems which the College set in place involved action at several levels and these remain in operation at the University today. These procedures set one model for the supervision of research students and for the support of their supervisors. The principal features of the University of Luton systems are outlined below.

Executive

The research degree mechanisms are managed by a small, four-member, team (the research executive) with clear responsibilities. The director of research is responsible to the University's academic board for the effective operation of the management and quality assurance systems for research degrees. The research supervisors' coordinator is responsible for supervisor training and serves as a general source of advice and support for all those supervising research degree students. The research students' tutor has the primary role of acting as an additional support to all research students and for monitoring the students' perceptions of the research degree programmes. The assistant academic registrar (research) provides a professional administrative support to all the institution's research procedures including those concerned with research degrees. Each of these four roles applies equally to all faculties of the University and to all research students and their supervisors.

In addition, the research executive is responsible for the production of a range of documents relating to research and to good practice in the supervision of research students.

Academic

The programme of each research student is overseen by Faculty and University committees which pay close attention to individual progress, particularly at initial registration and the point of transfer of registration from MPhil to PhD. At both Faculty and University levels, committees which deal directly with research degrees include external members drawn from other higher education institutions and other organizations.

Collaborative

A team approach to supervision was adopted to ensure that each student's programme and progress was overseen to successful completion by at least one supervisor with prior supervisory experience and two others. Since the local research community was (at least initially) relatively small, each student has an external supervisor who is able to lock the programme into the wider research community and into wider commercial, governmental or professional groups.

Training

Supervisor training is compulsory for all new supervisors and it is expected that the more experienced supervisors will also take part in the workshop sessions in order that the benefits of their experience may be shared with more novice colleagues. The training programme, organized by the research supervisors' coordinator, seeks to explain the University's administrative practices and to discuss the various roles which each supervisor must take on board during the period of study. Much of this training is informed by the model set out by Bennett and Knibbs (1986). This model identifies ten possible roles grouped into four key areas:

Process roles

1. The Bureaucrat – the supervisor is required to deal with the numerous forms required by the University and to ensure that regulations and procedures are adhered to, as the student progresses from enrolment through to examination.

2. The Initiator – the supervisor must initiate a number of events ranging from progress meetings through to the recommendation of an external examiner.

Academic roles

3. The Expert – the supervisor is required to provide expertise; for instance, directing the student to information, key literature and other researchers.

4. The Mentor – the supervisor should provide guidance on a range of matters relating to the student's work, including research design, methodology, analysis, development of concepts and dissemination of results.

5. The Innovator – the supervisor must, from time to time, stimulate the work of the student by adding new ideas. The aim here should be to develop the student's own powers of innovation and independent thought.

Interpersonal roles

6. The Friendly Helper – research can be lonely, frustrating and even depressing. The supervisor must help the student to overcome such difficulty by providing friendly support.

7. The Motivator – this role builds on that of the friendly helper by stimulating the student to see the value of the work undertaken. The need to provide praise where this is justified cannot be underestimated.

Validation roles

8. The Stern Critic – the supervisor must challenge the research student in order to develop the skills associated with defending the work. Critical appraisal of the research is essential if the student is to develop into a professional researcher.

9.   The Evaluator – the research student must be assisted in the evaluation of the work planned, in progress and completed. Realistic timetables and programmes of activity are central to satisfactory progress and the supervisor should ensure that the student's plan of work is achievable. Evaluation of and feedback on drafts of the thesis are essential if the research student is to achieve the required standards of competence in the presentation of research outcomes.

10. The Judge – the supervisor has a responsibility for a number of judgements which are crucial to the research student's progress through the University's procedures including registration, transfer from MPhil to PhD and finally submission of the completed thesis.

Although these models of the role of the supervisor inform the content of the supervisors' development programme, practicalities, of necessity, lead to a focusing of attention on the key stages of the research student's time with the university:

● Recruitment, selection and enrolment.

● Establishment of the student within the University and with a programme of activities.

● Development of agreed research protocols and topics to be investigated. Since formal registration is subject to approval by both faculty and University, the supervisors' programme includes close reference to the registration requirements and seeks to provide an understanding of what is required of the student at this stage.

● Transfer of registration from MPhil to PhD. This is not automatic and the student is required to provide oral and written reports. Again, the supervisors' programme seeks to provide an understanding of what is required to satisfy both the academic and administrative requirements at this stage.

● Support through the research and the establishment of standards appropriate to the desired degree. This includes debate and discussion of such issues as the differences between the MPhil and PhD degrees and the nature of originality.

● Preparation for final submission and defence of the thesis in a *viva voce* examination.

The principal mechanism through which the supervisors' programme operates is a short intensive course held at the start of each academic year, followed by a series of monthly supervisors' workshops which focus on specific issues. The programme is flexible and there is opportunity for additional topics of concern to be added at the request of students, supervisors or the research executive. For example, additional topics for 1994/95 have included an examination of the special constraints and concerns of those responsible for the supervision of staff candidates and a debate on the intellectual property rights associated with the research students' work.

EXPERIENCE AND PROCEDURES ELSEWHERE

The model set out above for the University of Luton provides one approach to supervisor support and development. Other institutions utilize other models and approaches.

A short survey sent to all UK universities in the summer of 1994 and addressed to the Pro-Vice Chancellor (Research) sought to establish the variety of approaches adopted to support new supervisors. From the 58 institutions which replied, the following points are worthy of note:

- A formal supervisor training programme was only compulsory in 14 institutions. However, in many more supervisor training programmes are available.

- Most institutions (47 of the 58) have a publication which outlines the roles and responsibilities of supervisors.

- Two-thirds of institutions have a code of practice on the supervision of research students.

- Half the institutions stated that there was a named individual with responsibility for provision of on-going support for supervisors.

The survey also requested copies of documentation relating to the support of supervisors of research students and the students themselves. Common practices which emerged repeatedly include:

- Several universities require all those new to supervision to work alongside a more experienced colleague who can be deemed to hold a mentor role. Sole supervision varies from being the normal practice through to never being allowed (as at the University of Luton).

- Recommendations are provided by several universities to supervisors on the minimum frequency with which supervisor(s) and student should meet. It should be noted that there is no consensus among universities concerning this minimum frequency (for instance University A suggests that two to three hours supervision per week is needed, while University B suggests a minimum of one meeting per month). Some universities use only rather vague terms such as 'supervisors must maintain *regular* contact with their students'.

- While some universities utilize a common approach for all faculties and departments, others adopt different overseeing and support procedures in the different academic areas. This is generally justified on the different needs of the various disciplines.

- Several universities have based their advice to supervisors on the booklet, *Research Student and Supervisor: An Approach to Good Supervisory Practice* (SERC, 1992) and to a lesser extent on similar booklets published by the ESRC and CVCP.

- It is recognized that the workload associated with good supervision can be considerable; as a consequence some universities impose a maximum number of students to be supervised by a single member of staff. However there is no consensus on the maximum number (University C states a maximum of ten FTE students per supervisor, University D suggests between four and six as a norm).

- For a significant number of research students and their supervisors, the sole source of published guidance (within their university) is the document which lists those regulations relevant to research degrees. For the most part these do little more than provide details of the administrative procedures.

- The amount (and quality) of documented advice given to new supervisors varies considerably (University E provides just a single A4 page while each faculty of University F publishes its own detailed advice and guidance).

It is recognized increasingly that while some individuals instinctively provide good support and supervision, others are less able to do so; this parallels the fact that some people are natural teachers and lecturers while others, despite their subject knowledge-base, struggle with aspects of delivery and student motivation. The idea of a standardized national programme of training for university teachers of undergraduates has never gained significant acceptance since the nature of our university sector is diverse. Similarly there are equivalent differences in the nature of the postgraduate research programmes within UK universities and hence with the supervision requirements.

The differences which exist between institutions offer one dimension in which to consider the issues but an alternative approach could be to focus on the needs of specific disciplines, say by establishing separate programmes for humanities and engineering staff. While there are certain elements of supervision and hence support requirements between disciplines not least those typified by the differences between laboratory-based students and others, the basic models of supervisory requirements (as described earlier) hold true for all disciplines and all institutions. I support the view that there are great benefits from cross-discipline developmental programmes since examples from a wide range of subjects and approaches to research serve to illustrate (to possibly very sceptical colleagues) that most, if not all, the crucial supervisory concerns are common to all.

CONCLUDING COMMENT

The survey (and the conference workshop at the SEDA conference in Worthing, November 1994) serve to illustrate that there is significant variation in current conditions of support for new supervisors and it is clear that many long-established universities might need to improve significantly their levels of support and published guidance to supervisors, if required to be judged to the criteria faced by the then Luton College of Higher Education in early 1993.

For these long-established institutions to merely rest on their laurels is not a viable possibility. The 1987 ESRC Report of the Inquiry on Submission Rates showed that submissions within four years were achieved by fewer than 20 per cent of ESRC and British Academy students in the social sciences and humanities and by less than 50 per cent of students supported by the MRC, NERC or SERC (Winfield, 1987).

The conference workshop concurred with the conclusions reached by the Universities Staff Development Unit report on staff development in relation to research (USDU, 1994), which recommended training for all supervisors, mentoring arrangements between experienced and novice supervisors, development of clear codes of practice on supervision arrangements and training in the management implications of research student supervision.

REFERENCES

Bennett, R and Knibbs, J (1986) 'Researching for a higher degree: The role(s) of the supervisor', *Management Education and Development*, 17, 2, 137–45.

SERC (1992) *Research Student and Supervisor: An approach to good supervisory practice*, Science and Engineering Research Council, Swindon.

USDU (1994) *Staff Development in Relation to Research*, Occasional Green Paper No 6, The UK Universities Staff Development Unit, Sheffield.

Winfield, G (1987) *The Social Science PhD: The ESRC inquiry on submission rates*, Economic and Social Research Council, Swindon.

Chapter 15

Enabling Student Learning Through Innovative Assessment

Liz McDowell

INTRODUCTION

Assessment as a means of enabling learning would seem a strange idea to some people, including some of our students. Although from an educational perspective we might argue that assessment is an integral part of learning, it is often viewed as a means of certifying or verifying the outcomes at the end of a process of learning. Students may see assessment simply as a requirement to demonstrate what they have learnt by sitting an exam, writing an essay or preparing a laboratory report. Nevertheless, assessment does have a strong influence on the way students behave and approach their learning, as much research into student learning in HE has shown (for example, Miller and Parlett, 1974).

This impact on students is one compelling reason for taking care with assessment. In addition, most theories of learning place strong emphasis on the role of feedback and this is one function which can be fulfilled by assessment. Most means of assessment involve presenting or communicating what the learner knows or can do and this in itself is an important part of learning. Some would argue that learning is not complete if it cannot be communicated coherently to someone else. New means of assessment are now in widespread use in HE and innovations such as assessment based on group projects, or portfolios, mean that assessment is not so much a one-off event or product but is integrated with a process of learning and to some extent inseparable from it.

For all these reasons, we need to pay careful attention to the way in which assessment is designed, the methods, the criteria used to judge students' work, and the ways in which marks are awarded. These are all mechanisms for enabling or promoting the kind of learning that we believe to be desirable.

THE IMPACT OF ASSESSMENT PROJECT

In the 'Impact of assessment' project at the University of Northumbria, we have undertaken a series of case studies of innovative assessment largely from the student perspective. Using interviews, questionnaires, observation and documentary evidence, we have been investigating what kinds of learning are being enabled and what factors seem to help and hinder learning.

Initially we defined innovative assessment according to the technique being used. A whole host of techniques are now common in HE, including group-based assessment; diaries, logs and journals; projects; oral assessment; assessment of skills or competences; profiles; portfolios; non-conventional exams; non-conventional writing tasks; simulations and role play; and assessment of experiential learning. There are also many excellent guides to the use of these methods (Brown *et al.*, 1994; Gibbs *et al.*, 1992). What we aimed to do was to begin to illuminate whether these innovative techniques were genuinely innovatory in the sense of improving student learning and avoiding some of the problems surrounding traditional approaches to assessment.

The five case studies used as a basis for this chapter included: a self-assessment exercise in applied statistics; a professional practice simulation with self- and peer assessment in a Built Environment subject; a Business Studies group case study project; a data presentation poster exercise with peer assessment on a social science course; and an open-book exam in systems methodology. Despite the variety of approaches, we were able to draw out some general issues about the impacts of such approaches on student learning.

WHAT KINDS OF LEARNING WERE ENABLED BY THESE APPROACHES?

Deep approach to learning

In our case studies we found most students attempting to take a deep rather than a surface approach to their learning although the level of outcomes of the learning varied between individuals. Most students tried to make sense of what they were learning. There was active engagement, shown, for example, by students trying to apply ideas from the course to new contexts such as the Business Studies case study, or by students creating their own over-arching structure to the topics covered by the Systems Methodology course in preparation for the open-book exam. Students were encouraged by the nature of some of the tasks set to relate their knowledge and skills to 'real-world' contexts and to draw on and integrate learning from a variety of subjects and sources. These are all characteristics of students taking a deep approach to their learning (Ramsden, 1992 pp.38–61). There were fewer examples of students taking a surface approach, that is, aiming to simply produce what was required for assessment in an unreflective way, or concentrating on repeating or re-hashing their notes. Students themselves could feel this difference between 'really learning something' or 'really understanding' and the requirements, as they perceived them, of some traditional forms of assessment such as exams for, 'regurgitation' or 'going through a set procedure'.

Intrinsic motivation

The kinds of innovative assessment we studied appeared to generate intrinsic motivation amongst students. They were interested in the activities they were involved in, they worked hard and felt a sense of ownership in what was produced. A real-world emphasis, the opportunity to work with other students and being involved in 'something different' all seemed to contribute to this high level of motivation. It can be contrasted sharply with the extrinsic motivation which can derive from the threat associated with some forms of assessment. In these examples the 'carrot' of involvement in a worthwhile and meaningful task tended to loom larger than the 'stick' of having to achieve a certain level of marks. At the end of the assessment there was a sense of satisfaction in what had been achieved rather than simply a sense of relief that it was over.

Skills development

None of our assessment tasks were simply about the development and manipulation of academic knowledge. Each one contained an intention to develop and assess students' skills – both subject-specific skills and what are normally termed 'personal transferable skills' such as communication or interpersonal skills. Our observations and discussions with students indicated that they had opportunities for development across a range of subject-specific or professional skills, and personal transferable skills such as written, oral and visual communication, interpersonal skills, negotiation, project planning and time management, and these opportunities were highly valued by students.

Evaluation of own learning

Students were encouraged by these assessment methods to become better able to reflect on and evaluate their own work and performance. Self- and peer assessment obviously made a particular contribution to this, but there were other examples including the requirement in one case to write a commentary on team work. Another relevant factor was that in every case students received clear guidance about what was expected of them and how they would be judged. They were given, or involved in negotiating, assessment criteria. This led some students to realize that assessment was not such a mysterious and unchallengable process as they had supposed and that they could be involved in it. The greater clarity and openness than is the norm, plus the very fact that the assessment differed from the conventional, may in itself have prompted some students to give more consideration than they usually did to what was required and how they were performing.

Flexibility and student choice

In all of these examples students had some flexibility and choice and a number of decisions to make about the work they undertook for assessment. Initially, choice of topic was fairly limited. For example, the Business Studies case studies and the topics for the data presentation exercise were allocated to groups. Nevertheless, students had a large degree of flexibility in how they went about the tasks allocated and the roles they adopted within their groups. Freedom to make choices and organize their own work did seem to be a positive factor in student learning.

WHAT KINDS OF PROBLEMS AROSE IN RELATION TO LEARNING?

Methods of organization to obtain fairness

Practical, organizational issues can easily be considered 'good enough' by lecturers when they adopt a new form of assessment, but students are acutely aware of any opportunities for unfairness. In some of our examples students believed that there were opportunities for cheating in self- and peer marking or cases where it was not taken seriously, because the controls were not sufficiently rigorous. Another student concern arose when individuals or groups received differential or misleading information from lecturers about assessment, or when requirements were changed at short notice. Where students or groups of students worked on different tasks or topics, inevitably some were seen as more difficult than others and if students did not feel that this was taken into account in some way, they could feel unfairly treated. It is always possible to tighten up on procedures but this last aspect of 'unfairness' is more difficult to tackle.

The limitations of flexibility and realism

It may seem from the issues that these methods of assessment were in some sense too innovative. However, in other respects students found them not innovative enough. Some students would have preferred more choice and flexibility. They felt that they would have learned more if they had been allowed to pursue their own interests or strengths to a greater extent. The allocation of specific topics or defined ways of undertaking tasks reduced the motivation and effort made by some.

Students welcomed assessment which was more realistic or at least less artificial than the conventional closed-book exam, but they then criticized the assessment for not being realistic enough in reflecting what would happen in the 'real world'. This criticism arose in a variety of ways but frequently in relation to team work. Students felt that many of the interpersonal problems, such as non-contribution, which they experienced would not happen in a working situation due to the sanctions available in that context. Many of us who have been part of teams at work might wish to disagree, but nevertheless lack of perceived realism was a demotivating factor for a number of students.

Time and stress

A common aim of changes to assessment practice is to reduce unnecessary levels of stress and anxiety arising from conventional assessment methods. However, we found students reported levels of stress and anxiety from working on long-term assignments which seemed to be counter-productive. Students acknowledged that some of the pressures were of their own making, due to poor time management, but we must bear in mind that some approaches to learning and assessment demand much time and effort from students. Part-time students may find it particularly difficult because of their limited study time and many of our full-time students now have external responsibilities such as families, homes and jobs which may make them less 'full-time' than they used to be. Lack of time to complete some tasks to their own satisfaction left a number of students feeling that they had missed an opportunity to fully get to grips with their learning.

The allocation of marks

Lecturers sometimes claim that it's the learning not the marks at the end which really counts. Up to a point students agree, but marks are nevertheless very important to them and they are disappointed when what they perceive as valuable learning and good work is apparently not rewarded by the marks received. One problem in some of our examples was that students became so engrossed in the details of the learning tasks that they paid little attention to assessment requirements. For example, some of the Business Studies students became so involved in their case studies that they spent all their time 'getting it right' rather than preparing for an assessed group presentation – and received disappointing marks. Another problem was that students did not fully understand the assessment criteria and aims. For example, the students undertaking the data presentation poster exercise saw it as all about computer skills and presentation whereas the lecturer was also looking for skills of data analysis and interpretation and evaluating the needs of a particular audience.

In some cases it appeared that the assessment criteria and marking scheme could not fully encompass the learning that had taken place, so some aspects lacked credit. This may be a particular difficulty with innovative assessment where the range of outcomes being assessed is often diverse, including academic and professional knowledge, and a range of subject-specific, vocational and transferable skills. Lecturers often claimed to be assessing both product, such as a report or poster produced, and process, such as how well students worked together as a team; in reality, marks tended to be awarded very much on the standard of the product produced. When groups worked together, there was a conflict between using individuals' strengths and abilities to achieve a better product and enabling group members to learn and develop in those areas where they were weakest.

Lack of feedback

All students were concerned to receive useful feedback on their work to help them improve in future. Approaches involving self- and peer assessment were explicitly designed to assist them to judge their own work but where there was concentration on mark allocation rather than giving feedback, students felt an opportunity to enhance learning had been missed. While students did gain practice and experience in judging their own work and learning, they not unreasonably still placed a high value on feedback from their lecturers and lacked confidence in their own judgements. Lack of feedback during the course of an assignment or project being undertaken over a period of time was also felt to be a problem by some students and they believed that this made their learning much less effective.

LESSONS TO BE LEARNED

There are some clear lessons to be learnt from our study. Students can be enabled via the design of assessment to engage in deep learning, to find an intrinsic motivation and a sense of satisfaction in their learning, to develop a range of skills and become more aware of means of assessing and judging their performance. Realistic and active tasks are one element, but they also need to be tasks which require students to integrate and deepen their understanding. Collaboration with other students is also very helpful, whether it is via a team assignment or using some other means to encourage sharing of ideas and mutual support. The reduction of unnecessary stress and anxiety which often stem from conventional assessment methods is also helpful. However, we also have to ensure that the time and effort which students will devote to the assessment is reasonable and in proportion to their overall workloads.

The success of these approaches is likely to be greatly enhanced by rigorous procedures which enhance the reliability and validity of assessment and ensure fair treatment for students. There needs to be planning to cope with the potential problems which may arise, as far as these can be foreseen, just as we have ways of dealing with the situation if, say, a student misses an exam. The student voice is useful here as a reminder to us. For example, lecturers assessing via group assignments where the majority of groups work well together on most occasions may not consider that the occasional group which breaks down invalidates the approach. Since we cannot offer the same restricted situation as in an exam room, openness and clarity need to be high priorities for innovative assessment so all those closely involved, including students, can build up trust and confidence in approaches used.

Many students could benefit from guidance, practice and training in relation to conventional assessment methods but their needs become more obvious when new methods are introduced. The most obvious example from our case studies was that while self- and peer assessment yielded a number of benefits, students needed more opportunities to undertake it and guidance in doing so if it was to achieve its full potential. The same may apply to a number of skill areas, for example, skills in oral presentation, team work, negotiation or project planning.

The assessment criteria and the way in which marks are allocated are obviously of key importance. Where a range of outcomes is envisaged, it is important to clarify how the outcomes will be assessed and what weighting the different elements will receive in terms of marks. One particular problem is the balance between assessment of outcomes or *product* and assessment of *process*. We would argue that in many cases the learning process is poorly assessed. This is perhaps because assessment in HE tends to be very much about maintaining and certifying standards rather than monitoring student progress and giving credit for development. It is possible that there needs to be some formative assessment focusing on process issues which does not count towards a final result. Where skills are used during the process of an assessment task, valid ways of assessing them need to be carefully considered rather than simply making assumptions that, for example, a good team report necessarily results from the deployment of a high standard of team work skills.

Feedback is of key importance for learning and therefore all methods of assessment will be enhanced by the provision of useful feedback to learners. Marks in themselves are not necessarily useful feedback. Students tend to place most faith in feedback from their lecturers, but the time available for lecturers to give feedback to individual students is increasingly scarce. Time-saving ways of giving feedback need to be adopted and we may also have to develop students' confidence and ability in providing feedback to each other and judging their own work.

Finally, innovative assessment is likely to be most useful in enabling learning if it allows for student flexibility, choice and individual needs. Sometimes assessment is a hindrance in this respect when students feel under pressure to produce a good outcome rather than trying to develop in areas where they know themselves to be weak. We also found that there was sometimes a mismatch between an assessment task and the level of knowledge and interests of the students involved in it. The task might be appropriate for a course of that level and scope but it was not an appropriate next step for the individual students involved.

CONCLUSIONS

Innovative assessment may introduce some new techniques, but it remains very much within the conventional framework of assessment in HE. However radical these approaches may appear in some quarters, they are evolutionary rather than revolutionary. Within the current system there are limits to how far innovative assessment can develop and some strong challenges may be met.

The possibility that innovative assessment encourages students to take a deep approach to their learning and foster intrinsic interest in their studies is widely welcomed. The aim to promote and assess personal and vocational skills and the potential requirement to assess the process of learning in addition to its outcomes would be more controversial. To attune assessment to developmental needs of individual students and give credit for individual progress would be a major shift in HE which has always tended to focus on notionally fixed standards of achievement. HE also places a high value on rigour and reliability in assessment and new approaches may have to prove their case in these respects, in a situation constrained by reductions in resources.

Innovative assessment does have the distinct advantage that it tends to generate debate and discussion about the fundamentals of assessment – what is really being assessed? Is this what should be being assessed? Is the assessment equitable and fair? What are its side-effects? In many cases, this debate also involves students. All this increases the possibility of developing open, reliable and valid assessment which enables students to learn rather than simply perform.

REFERENCES

Brown, S, Rust, C and Gibbs, G (1994) *Strategies for diversifying assessment in Higher Education*, Oxford Centre for Staff Development, Oxford.

Gibbs, G *et al.* (1992) *Assessing More Students. Teaching More Students*, Series No 4, Oxford Centre for Staff Development, Oxford.

Miller, C M L and Parlett, M (1974) *Up to the Mark: A study of the examination game*, SRHE, Guildford.

Ramsden, P (1992) *Learning to Teach in Higher Education*, Routledge, London.

Chapter 16

Using Practical Assessment to Support Student Learning: A Case Study

Nick Sutcliffe

INTRODUCTION

The increasing need to develop and assess a wider range of clinical skills in trainee podiatrists (chiropodists) has led to moves within the podiatry division away from the traditional single-case practical examination in the direction of a more eclectic and comprehensive style of assessment. The objective structured clinical examination (OSCE) has been widely used within medical disciplines but its potential as a learning and assessment tool may not have been fully exploited in other disciplines which require the development and assessment of practical skills. This chapter outlines the introduction of the OSCE and suggests that many of the benefits conferred by this assessment format may transfer readily into other subject areas. Following trial implementations in 1992 and 1993 (where it was used in parallel with traditional practical examinations), the OSCE was recognized as a valuable method for diagnosing both individual and whole-group learning difficulties. This allowed the course design team to re-evaluate their approach to the teaching of particular topics and target teaching resources and individual support in a more efficient manner. A comprehensive student evaluation produced overwhelming support for the format which was perceived as being fairer and more realistic than the original practical examination format.

WHAT IS AN OSCE?

The OSCE is the objective, structured, clinical examination. It has its origins in the mid-1970s where it was first used to assess the clinical skills of medical students at the University of Dundee (Harden *et al.*, 1975). The OSCE has also been used in a variety of other areas, to update and upgrade the clinical skills of general practitioners (Biran, 1991), to provide feedback to students (Black and Harden, 1986) and in assessing performance in non-clinical disciplines (Harden and Cairncross, 1980).

Typically, an OSCE consists of a number of small, finite tasks to be attempted by the student within a fixed time period; these are usually grouped together on a topic or subject basis. Each of these tasks occurs at a fixed location, known as a station; based on a review of current literature, a complete OSCE can include anywhere between ten and 25 stations. The number of stations used in an OSCE may depend upon:

- the time available for each station – longer time allocations for each station tend to be associated with fewer stations;

- the purpose and range of the examination – a broad summative end-of-year examination could be expected to be significantly longer than a narrow formative assessment aimed at skill development within a very specific area.

Some stations within the OSCE involve direct observation by an examiner to assess the student's performance, while for other stations, pen and paper are used to record the student's attempt to address the task at the station, and these sheets are collected for marking later. A signal, such as a bell or buzzer is used to mark the start and end of the time allocation for each station and may also be used to mark the start of any changeover time, allowing students to move between stations and to read any information relating to the task at the new station prior to commencing the task.

The OSCE has been shown to have a high degree of validity when compared with traditional methods of assessment (Woodburn and Sutcliffe, in press), although there may need to be further research to establish levels of reliability comparable to those of established assessment methodologies (Roberts and Norman, 1990).

Unlike many other forms of assessment where the final *product* is the principal (and sometimes the only) focus, in the OSCE the *process* can be the most important feature of the assessment. This means that the OSCE can be an important means of supporting student learning where it is used in a diagnostic or formative manner.

Emphasis is placed on the objectivity and structure of the assessment procedure, and this method has been used in non-clinical environments where it has been referred to as the OSPE, (with 'practical' in place of 'clinical'). The *objectivity* of the OSCE comes from its requirement that all participants complete an identical range of tasks, and usually the same examiner is used to assess all performances at a particular station or group of stations. The *structured* element of the assessment is derived from the uniform requirements for each station and, in designing the OSCE, staff can ensure that attention is paid to a broad range of skills and competences, rather than a very narrow sampling pattern as has often been the case with traditional methods of practical assessment. In the traditional scenario, the outcomes of a narrow practical assessment are extrapolated into areas that were not examined during the assessment process.

Key features of the OSCE are that it:

- allows the separate assessment of process and product through the observation of performance and the assessment of the end result;

- provides adequate sampling of skills and content to be tested;

- is an analytical approach to assessment;

- has a greater degree of objectivity than traditional forms of practical assessment;

- provides feedback to students and teachers (Harden & Cairncross, 1980).

WHAT CHANGES LED TO THE INTRODUCTION OF THE OSCE ONTO THE PODIATRY DEGREE COURSE?

For several years, the professional bodies responsible for conferring the licence to practice for podiatrists within the health services have specified not only the knowledge content of courses but also the format of the assessments which examine that knowledge base. The qualification (at two-year diploma level) was replaced three years ago by the award of a three-year ordinary degree; more recently this has evolved into a three-year honours degree award. The introduction of the new qualification at first degree level offered the opportunity to change the format of the assessment programme.

Under the previous system of practical assessment, each student was assessed on their clinical competences in treating two patients within a three-hour period. The student performances were assessed by means of an oral examination which lasted for approximately 20 minutes, and there was no formal requirement for the student to be the subject of any direct observation by the examiner during the period of the examination.

In the current undergraduate scheme, professional body representation takes place on the validating panel of the degree programme. The professional bodies retain an important role in ensuring that the core knowledge content which podiatrists need is maintained and updated as a requirement of The Professions Supplementary to the Medicine Act. These changes in requirements have led to the OSCE being introduced alongside (in the case of third/final-year students) the traditional practical assessment. Second and third year student groups currently undertake OSCEs which are seen as an important factor in the development of students' clinical skills as well as being a means of measuring clinical competence.

WHAT IS THE FORMAT OF A TYPICAL OSCE IN PODIATRY, AND WHAT HAVE BEEN THE IMPLICATIONS OF ITS INTRODUCTION FOR BOTH STUDENTS AND STAFF?

All the OSCE assessments take place within a purpose-built clinic within the school and most of the patients are members of the public from the Huddersfield area. The podiatry clinic consists of a large central area divided into 28 small booths (similar in appearance to those found in the accident and emergency units of many hospitals) with an additional number of small treatment rooms on the outside of this central area. The plan of the clinic as illustrated in Figure 16.1 shows its organization in the case of a typical 24-station OSCE.

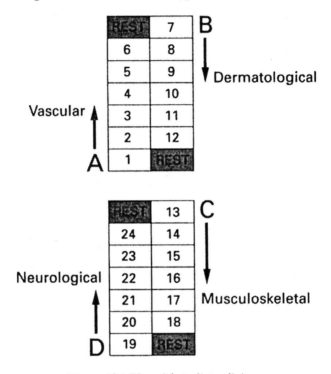

Figure 16.1 *Plan of the podiatry clinic*

The clinic is divided into four areas of clinical specialism with six stations in each area. The clinical specialisms are (i) the neurological system, (ii) the vascular system, (iii) dermatology and (iv) the musculoskeletal system.

Each station consists of a task requiring completion during a five-minute period, followed by a one-minute changeover period to allow for the collection and distribution of answer sheets and to allow students to rotate between stations. Students were graded under three headings: task accomplished, task not accomplished, or task not attempted. Performances at each station were graded against a set of pre-specified criteria which were devised by staff and these criteria are not (at the time of writing) made explicit prior to the OCSE.

Examples of the types of tasks used included taking a patient's clinical history and making a diagnosis of a patient's condition (both stations observed by examiners). A number of patients who visit the clinic on a regular basis for podiatric treatment have kindly offered to help with the OSCE by allowing students to take their clinical histories and perform diagnoses on them. Other stations involve, for example, watching a short (30-second) video of a patient walking and diagnosing gait abnormalities, or examining a number of photographs and slides of fungal infections of the foot and prescribing a range of possible treatments.

To illustrate the process in greater detail, one can consider the situation of a student entering the clinic at the first of the musculoskeletal stations (ie, station 13 in Figure 16.1). The student moves to the station on the first signal (a bell or buzzer) and then has the remainder of a one-minute period to read the requirements of the task at that station. After the second signal, a bell or buzzer sounds to indicate the start of the five-minute task completion period and the student begins the task. This could involve, for example, the examination of a number of x-ray plates of a patient's foot, with each one having been taken from a different perspective. The student is then required to (i) write a concise and reasoned diagnosis for the condition presented (ii) propose a remedial course of treatment for the patient. After five minutes have elapsed, the bell or buzzer sounds for a third time to signal the end of the allotted time allowed for that station and the student moves on to the next station (in this example, number 14). The process is then repeated until all the students have visited all the stations.

A recent innovation currently being developed in the department which it is intended to be used for some of the stations consists of an interactive multimedia software package based on student responses to different clinical conditions. The interactive nature of the program enables it to develop a prognosis of the possible consequences of both appropriate and inappropriate treatments, and to present the student with a report of the patient's changing clinical condition.

The OSCE does make very intensive use of staff resources in terms of both the preparation prior to the OSCE and staffing arrangements during the examination. An item bank of suitable OSCE stations is currently under development, and a panel has been established within the departmental staff to assess the suitability of tasks. This panel also has responsibility for overseeing the trial of each new task to ensure its adequacy and feasibility before adding it to the item bank.

The need for adequate staffing has led to the introduction of some students (usually from the first year of the course) and technical staff being involved in routine tasks (such as the collection and distribution of materials, rewinding videotape, etc.), and if the examination is eventually to be used as the sole summative practical assessment for final year students, difficulties presented in this area will require additional thought being given to the management of different groups and the OSCE to maintain the objectivity and avoid 'contamination' of the student helpers. This problem may become less of an issue as a larger item bank is developed, but recording which students helped with which OSCE and which tasks they were exposed to could be a potential difficulty in the longer term if not taken account of at this stage.

The nature of the examination also makes the OSCE a very intensive experience for the students, staff examiners and patients, so a small number of rest stations have been built into the OSCE to give participants a break within the examination period – which in this case lasts for almost three hours. Many of the student comments in the evaluation reflect the intensity and thoroughness of the process.

As well as these practical implications, OSCE has had implications for teaching staff in that areas of weakness within the teaching programme have been identified. The neurological specialism was identified as an area that needed attention in this way and this has led to additional resources in terms of staff teaching time being reallocated to this area to provide a number of specialist neurological clinics. It was also noticeable that prior to assessing an OSCE, several members of staff were observed 'brushing-up' on their own clinical skills!

HOW WAS THE OSCE EVALUATED AND WHAT DID STUDENTS AND STAFF PERCEIVE AS BEING THE ADVANTAGES AND DISADVANTAGES OF THE OSCE?

Shortly after completing the OSCE, (but prior to receiving their individual results) the students were asked to complete an evaluation form which focused their attention on different aspects of the exam. All of the questions in this version of the evaluation were devised by staff, but it is intended that as more evaluations are conducted, the range of questions used will take greater account of any overall trends in perception emerging from the evaluation forms. This evaluation was conducted with a group of 24 final-year students who had also experienced a trial practical examination under the traditional format. The results are shown in Table 16.1.

Table 16.1 *Student evaluation results*

Questions	Strongly agree % (Count)	Agree % (Count)	Neutral % (Count)	Disagree % (Count)	Strongly disagree % (Count)
Q.1 I was made fully aware of the nature of the examination	29.1 (7)	70.8 (17)	0	0	0
Q.2 The practical tasks that you were asked to do in the examination reflected those taught in the module	29.1 (7)	70.8 (17)	0	0	0

Questions	Strongly agree % (Count)	Agree % (Count)	Neutral % (Count)	Disagree % (Count)	Strongly disagree % (Count)
Q.3 The theoretical aspects of the exam reflected those taught in the module	20.8 (5)	62.5 (15)	16.7 (4)	0	0
Q.4 The five-minute time at each station was adequate	25.0 (6)	62.5 (15)	12.5 (3)	0	0
Q.5 The one-minute time between each station was adequate	16.7 (4)	79.2 (19)	4.2 (1)	0	0
Q.6 The instructions given at each station were clear and unambiguous	12.5 (3)	45.8 (11)	29.2 (7)	12.5 (3)	0
Q.7 The tasks that you were asked to perform at each station were fair	29.2 (7)	62.5 (15)	8.3 (2)	0	0
Q.8 The stations progressed in a logical manner	29.2 (7)	70.8 (17)	0	0	0

Two open questions were also included on the evaluation form which invited students to comment on positive and negative aspects of the exam:

Q.9 What positive things can you say about the exam?

'The exam was fair' (18 comments)
'A wide range of knowledge/clinical skills was covered' (17 comments)
'The exam tested all-round knowledge' (2 comments)
'The exam was well organized' (2 comments)
'The exam flowed well (good structure)' (1 comment)
'The exam reduced chances of me failing' (1 comment)
'Less stressful' (1 comment)
'Allowed me to compensate for weak areas' (1 comment)
'It was a good exam' (1 comment)
'It reassured/highlighted certain topics that I am weak on' (1 comment)

'My problem areas have been identified' (1 comment)
'It was good that there were the same examiners for all students'
(1 comment)
'It wasn't an intimidating exam' (1 comment)

Q.10 What negative things can you say about the exam?

'I did not know how much information was needed in the 5 minutes'
(4 comments)
'Some instructions were not clear' (4 comments)
'I was unsure as to what clinical tests to do in the five minutes'
(1 comment)
'I needed more time' (1 comment)
'I found it very stressful' (1 comment)
'I need more revision in neurology' (1 comment)

Two further questions were:

Q.11 I would rate my own performance as	Very good % (count)	Good % (count)	Average % (count)	Poor % (count)	Very poor % (count)
	0	0	79.1 (19)	20.8 (5)	0

Q.12 Would you like to sit this style of examination in future	Yes % (count)		No % (count)	
	100 (24)		0 (0)	

CONCLUSIONS ON THE EVALUATION OF THE OSCE

The student comments were, on the whole, very positive about the examination, and the themes of fairness and objectivity are highlighted by many of the respondents. Comments on the clarity of instructions at individual stations prompted staff to revisit those stations to try, where possible, to reduce any ambiguity. The responses also suggested that student learning across a wide range of clinical disciplines had been enhanced, and that the students' awareness of their own learning deficiencies had been raised in a way that was both structured and diagnostic so as to facilitate remediation. Negative comments related to the time limitations at each station, and the key to reducing some of these anxieties may be for staff to ensure that the students are well prepared for the examination, not only in terms of its content, but also in terms of the demands of the format (for example the need to be concise, the importance of prioritizing different elements within the five-minute period for each station, etc).

On the whole, the students' rating of their own performance in the examination was below that of the clinical staff, who rated the performance of this group as being in the average to good categories rather than the average to poor classifications that the students gave themselves.

If the whole process is viewed within a broader context, the self-diagnostic and remediation aspects of the OSCE can be seen as key elements in developing the role of students as autonomous learners. It also suggests that using appropriate and developmental forms of assessment (such as the OSCE) could be a significant factor in the empowerment of learners.

In addition to the formal student evaluation of the OSCE, a number of informal discussions also took place with staff and with students from several different groups and these raised the following issues.

Patient fatigue was seen to be an issue – by the time that patients were being seen by (say) student 15, several examiners noted that many patients were giving the students their clinical history regardless of the quality and relevance of the student's questioning. Although this can be taken account of by the examiner/observer, it can be a threat to the objectivity of the assessment process, especially where a diagnosis is called for. Examiners also noted that in some cases the patients actually changed the description of their symptoms as the examination progressed. Staff working at these stations suggested that this was probably as a result of the onset of boredom in the patients.

Scripting' of patient responses may be seen as threatening the reality (the validity) of the assessment exercise, and carefully designed additional preparation and selection of the patients (many of whom are elderly and/or infirm) may help to reduce this to some extent.

Temporal disorientation was experienced by many students especially in the later stages of the examination. Several students became confused as to whether a particular buzzer signalled the start of a station or the start of a changeover period. This difficulty is relatively easily overcome through the use of different buzzers or bells to represent different events.

Students who had taken part in more than one OSCE suggested that the starting point (vascular system, neurological system, etc) could make a difference to their performance depending on their response to particular specialties. As it would not be practical to start everyone at the same point, a pen-and-paper 'warm-up' exercise might be useful in helping to reducing this factor. As more data emerge from more OSCEs it may be possible to find out if there is a correlation between starting point and performance, although in the current OSCE format the student's starting point is not recorded.

HOW COULD THE OSCE BE ADAPTED FOR USE WITHIN OTHER DISCIPLINES?

While our experience in using the OSCE format suggests that there are significant benefits in terms of its ability to enhance student learning, there are also limitations and potential difficulties which need to be recognized, and these require consideration prior to adopting this form of assessment. In particular, the following questions need to be addressed by any potential user as they have been identified both in the current literature and also by the podiatry department as being the most problematic areas.

What is the purpose of the assessment?

- How does the OSCE fit in with other assessments that we already do? Does the OSCE integrate well with other parts of the assessment package for the course?

- How will the results of the assessment or any other outcomes be used? Are they to be used within a formative and diagnostic or summative and judgemental context?

- How are grades and criteria derived? They could be formulated in a number of ways: by staff alone, by negotiation between staff and students, or by the students themselves. Linked to this, are the criteria which are to be used implicit or explicit?

What are the resource implications?

- What resources are currently available and what additional resources (if any) will be needed? This could include factors such as the availability of suitable rooms, the availability of adequate time for the preparation of students, staff and rooms prior to the examination, and examination staffing implications, in terms of both technical and clinical staffing.

What is the nature of the practical skills to be assessed?

- Is it possible, with relative ease, to devise a number of stations that cover the range of practical skills to be assessed? Can sufficient tasks which take, for example, five or ten minutes to complete, be devised, or are the skills so disparate in their nature that they would not easily fit this format? Could any larger task be broken down into a number of smaller, discrete and equal-length tasks?

- Is there a significant potential for the development of a range of alternate tasks for each station? Is there a very limited range of potential tasks or could an item bank of suitable tasks for each station be developed?

Developing the OSCE or OSPE

If some of the difficulties raised in the previous section prove to be insurmountable and preclude the use of the full assessment, it may still be possible to utilize some benefits of the OSCE (see p.167) assessment process. Examples of appropriate activities to achieve this could include:

- Allowing students to develop OSCE exercises and trialing them with their peers. This focuses the students on the need to work within the confines of a (staff-generated) framework and encourages them to think of what evidence *they* would generate to demonstrate that an individual has acquired a particular skill.

- Encouraging the students to work in small groups to produce a mini-OSCE within a specific and confined clinical area. This process could become essentially iterative in that the students could be encouraged to refine their mini-OSCE, which could then be used with students from other small groups engaged in a similar activity on a reciprocal basis. Involving students in teaching and assessing each others' practical skills could be followed by a short plenary session in which the tutor(s) ensure that the required elements have been adequately covered to a satisfactory standard by each small group.

There are several potential benefits for students and staff in undertaking these exercises.

- Students will be able to gain a better understanding of the assessment process which may help to address the concerns expressed in the evaluation of those students who had difficulty in selecting appropriate diagnostic tests or treatments within the time allowed.

- The nature of the exercises encourages students to engage in both self- and peer assessment. If the activity is framed in a developmental and supportive manner with appropriate preparation and summary sessions, there is the potential to encourage the students to also learn from the *content* of the mini-OSCE. The clinical staff can act in a peripatetic, supporting role, moving between the student groups. This can produce savings on formal teaching time elsewhere and so the activity replaces part of the formal teaching programme rather than simply adding to an already full teaching programme.

- Any particularly successful OSCE exercises which emerge from the mini-OSCEs can be added to the item bank for use in future OSCEs with other groups of students.

Acknowledgments

I would like to acknowledge assistance in preparing this chapter from the staff, students and patients from the podiatry department at the University of Huddersfield, and the participants at the SEDA conference workshop on 'Assessing practical skills'.

REFERENCES

Biran, L A (1991) 'Self-assessment and learning through GOSCE (Group Objective Structured Clinical Examination', *Medical Education*, 25, 6, 475–9.

Black, N M I and Harden, R M (1986) 'Providing Feedback on Clinical Skills by Using the Objective Structured Clinical Examinations', *Medical Education*, 20, 1, 48–52.

Harden, R M and Cairncross, R G (1980) 'The assessment of practical skills: the Objective Structured Practical Examination (OSPE)', *Studies in Higher Education*, 5, 2, 187–96.

Harden, R M, Stevenson, M, Downie, W W and Wilson, G M (1975) 'The assessment of clinical competence using Objective Structured Clinical Examinations', *British Medical Journal*, 1, 477.

Roberts, J and Norman, G (1990) 'Reliability and learning from the Objective Structured Clinical Examination', *Medical Education*, 24, 219–23.

Woodburn, J and Sutcliffe, N M (in press) 'The reliability, validity and evaluation of the Objective Structured Clinical Examination in podiatry', *Assessment and Evaluation in Higher Education*.

Conclusions

Sally Brown and Gina Wisker

Enabling student learning requires a consistent and strategic approach: however hard individual lecturers work on a small scale with their own students, an holistic approach is essential to ensure that universities are providing students with what they need. The following concluding thoughts, derived mainly from other contributing authors, offer a few suggestions for those who wish to adopt a reasoned and substructive strategy for student support:

- Universities which fail to provide adequate support for students will lose market share and will provide a poor service to their students.

- Unitized and modular courses require a higher degree of student support, especially in enabling effective and appropriate student choice.

- Students are often well able to support each other in their learning and by so doing, become more effective learners themselves.

- Enabling student learning is not a cheap or easy option. Universities and colleges that adopt a strategic approach are likely to be more effective at supporting students than those which leave provision to local departments or chance. Investments need to be made (of both money and resources) to assume student enablement.

- The increasing move towards Student Charters has given students a better idea of what kinds of services they are entitled to expect, while often at the same time outlining their responsibilities towards the institution.

- As curriculum delivery methods change, students will need increased support to enable them to make best use of flexible learning resources provided.

- Strategies to enable student learning are often transferable from subject to subject and context to context, as many of these chapters show.

- Students on non-traditional routes often require a higher level of support.

- Different methods of support are required for different kinds of students.

- No institution can hope to get it all right first time; enabling student learning is an ongoing dynamic process that requires continuing investment of resources, particularly staff, to ensure high quality support.

Universities which take account of these ideas and those put forward throughout this book, and put them into practice, can expect to see a high return on their investment.

Index